DON'T STAY A SECRET ™

GROW YOUR CONFIDENCE CREATING VIDEOS THAT GET VIEWS

Felicia H. Yap

DON'T STAY A SECRET ™
Grow Your Confidence Creating Videos That Get Views
By Felicia H. Yap

Published by Felicia H. Yap, founder of Reel Awesome Productions

www.reelawesome.com

Copy editing by Stephen Dutcher
Editorial editing by Lyndsie Barrie, Noreen Music, Ryan Sang, Julia Wong, Stephanie Lim, Yvonne Chapman, Mary Truong, Jennifer Vuong, Shawn Yap and Shane McQueen
Formatting by Shane Fielder of Samurai Innovation
Cover design by Cheryl Fielder of Samurai Innovation
Cover photo by Laurie Brown of
Laurie MacBrown Photography
Cover makeup and hair by Adrienne Furrie of
Adrienne Furrie Makeup

ISBN: 978-1-7780132-0-1 (Paperback edition)

First Edition

WHAT PEOPLE ARE SAYING

Calgary-based coach Kerri Cust was struggling to elevate her own videos to promote her business. She had enough of watching other content creators make videos with trending transitions and reached out to Felicia for help to figure out how she could do it too.

I took Felicia's Video Confidence Academy, and I got such good results. She was so informed, she provided such good support. The video and editing tips were unbelievable. It changed everything. Now it's so easy, I can do all these professional-type techniques in my own videos and everything on my phone. Felicia made it so easy. She gave us so many free resources to use. And now my videos just look so much better on my social media, everything looks so smooth and professional, and it was easy, and I even feel like I could teach other people how to do this. She's more than qualified, and I had such a positive experience I would definitely do the course again, and I highly, highly recommend it. It just took my videos to a whole new level. And I couldn't be happier. So, if you're thinking about doing the Video Confidence Academy course, I highly, highly recommend it.

– Kerri Cust

Ottawa-based Nicole Bourgeois was in the early stages of starting up her hypnosis business when she decided to take Felicia's Video Confidence Academy. She had virtually zero experience making videos. By the end of the group course, video creation was no longer daunting; she said it was like getting a new toy that was fun to play with.

Hi, my name is Nicole. Full transparency, I can't say I was 100% sure of what I was signing up for when I first reached out to Felicia. I was starting a new business. I knew I was going to have to incorporate video into my business somehow, whether that was long-form for my website or short-form for social media. Long-form I felt a little more prepared for, psychologically. But social media is a different beast entirely. Posting regularly and coming up with good content were not things I was finding it easy to wrap my head around. And these are the things that I really needed assistance with. So, when the course started, Felicia really laid everything out to us so that we knew what to expect from session to session. I learned about batching. I learned about transitions. I learned about apps that help me fix my mistakes so that I don't have to start over and over and over again. I learned how to have fun. I learned lots.

I really enjoyed working with Felicia. She's a really great teacher and has a lot of passion for what she does, and a lot of patience – a lot of patience with me. I have in fact completed the video that we initially discussed that I needed to do for my business. I have used many fewer ums.

So, thank you for that. I'm taking a little more time, and I feel a lot more confident about tackling what direction I need to go when it comes to what's next, on video, for Nicole. Thank you so much.

– Nicole Bourgeois

Jerilyn Wolstenholme is a Calgary-based professional organizer, and the owner of Please Organize My Life. She helps clients manage their time and possessions better. As a solopreneur, she wanted to learn how to shoot videos on her own to promote her business, and after personalized, one-on-one coaching with Felicia, she can do it.

I'm very grateful for Felicia's experience as she is helping me overcome some of the challenges associated with filming and social media videos. Her professional manner helped me learn some great practical tips to get me over the hump of starting to film and I would happily recommend her to any business owner needing support. Some of the specific things we worked on during our sessions were practical tips like remembering to smile more and how to prepare my body physically and emotionally for the presentation. After our session I was able to complete a video I needed for a rebranded website and her encouragement just helped me get it off my things-to-do list.

– Jerilyn Wolstenholme

For Andrew, Aurora and Gwyneth who make my heart sing and make every day magical because they're in the world.

TABLE OF CONTENTS

Introduction
A DENIAL DOES NOT MEAN DEFEAT

"Life is too short to waste time waiting for other people's approval on how you live it."
– Steve Maraboli

We all get judged. Someone may look at me on the front cover of this book and think "What could she possibly know about how to grow confident creating videos that get views?" Before you make your mind up about me, let me set the record straight. I have more than 20 years of experience in front of the camera and behind it. I'm a professional presenter that has delivered countless stories live to tens of thousands of people every day when I worked, at different times, as a news anchor, as a morning show co-host, as a reporter, and as a weather specialist working for CTV, a leading Canadian news network. I started shooting, editing, and producing videos when I was a kid, and made the leap to do it professionally when I became a video journalist, and now as the owner of the video production company Reel Awesome Productions. All my experience allows me to help teach you how to make videos with more impact and how you can show up as your best and brightest self on screen.

You may look at my experience and think "Being confident making videos and starring in them is easy for you, Felicia. How can I do it too?"

Well, my friend, I stepped away from my successful career as a broadcast journalist when I became a mom. I started over from scratch as a content creator, a videographer, and as a video confidence coach – building a following on social media – without a big company backing me up. I've been doing this for a long time, so I can testify making videos on your own can be complicated. But it doesn't have to be. With me as your guide, you have everything you need to start making videos right now! And now is the perfect time to start.

I did not always look or feel confident. I'm the daughter of hard-working immigrants from Singapore. I didn't look like most of the kids in my Calgary neighbourhood. I was also quiet, awkward, and nerdy. Growing up, my family lived paycheque to paycheque. The only new-to-me clothes I got came from older cousins who didn't want them anymore, and from a generous relative who bought my brothers and I back-to-school outfits every year. We didn't have much, but we didn't need much. One luxury item we did have was my dad's camcorder. From recording commercials plucked from my imagination to pretending to be a news anchor, playing around with that Sony Handycam brought a lot of magic into my world and allowed me to show a part of myself that I was too shy to share off screen.

Creating videos has been my happy place since I was little. And while my work ethic is innate, my ability to captivate an audience did not come automatically. I've made big mistakes and embarrassed myself in front of a lot of people. I've also never felt more alive than when I speak into a microphone in front of an audience. And that's how I learned this unshakable truth:

When you discover what makes your heart sing, you will find your purpose.

People can't get enough of watching videos – the hunger is insatiable. Video is the easiest way to build relationships and connect with people over social media, because you can show who you are. Not only can people *hear* your unique voice, but they can also *see* you at the same time, and *feel* your heart, your passion, your compassion, and what makes you the seriously amazing person that you are!

We crave connection and authenticity. I truly believe that when you show up from a genuine place and intentionally want to help others, creating videos will boost your impact, influence, and income.

REFLECTION EXERCISE ON HOW YOU FEEL ABOUT MAKING VIDEOS

If you've picked up this book, there's a very good chance that you're a high achiever with a valuable message and tons of knowledge that you'd love to share with the world. But let's be honest – there's also a good chance that the thought of getting in front of a camera to share that wisdom makes you break out in a cold sweat. I wager that trying to figure out how to shoot videos and use video editing apps stops you from recording the ideas in your head. I'll stop guessing now and ask you to answer a few questions honestly. Even with the best intentions, you might forget how you feel right now, so write your answers down here:

How do you feel about creating videos with yourself in them?

____

____

____

What has prevented you from doing it in the past?

____

____

____

Perhaps you've tried it once and didn't do it again. If so, why did you stop?

____

____

If you blame yourself, let me tell you the truth: it's NOT your fault. How can you expect to be good at it if you've never been taught it before?

This leads to more questions that I'd like you to answer:

Why do you want to use video?

____

____

____

Are you an innovator with a bright idea who dreams of making videos to teach, inspire or entertain? Are you an entrepreneur who believes video is the best way to promote your business? Or are you a professional who wants to spread your message on virtual stages? Put pen to paper. I promise that nailing down your purpose for using video will help you get the most out of this book.

____

____

____

Thanks for doing that. We'll look at your answers again later. The good news is video creation and showing up confidently on camera are both 100% learnable skills! As someone who in many ways is an introvert, it's safe to say that I've been where you are. But it's through my failures and triumphs that I've learned how to make videos the simple way and became confident presenting live to tens of thousands of people every day.

The exercises throughout this book are designed to help you take steps out of your comfort zone, to magnify your message, to clarify the stories you want to share, and to help you fall head over heels for video. And when that happens, I bet your audience will feel the same way about you. When you apply the principles of this book, not only will it help you become more confident on screen, it will also change the way you present yourself in person.

Almost everything between the covers of this book includes what I wish I knew when I started taking video creation seriously. Don't wait to finish reading this book before you actually start creating content. Answer the questions I ask and do the work. Put what you learn into practice. I'll be your guide and cheer you on, every step of the way.

Please don't judge this book by its cover alone. What you'll find within these pages are proven methods to look and feel confident in front of the camera, and behind it, along with the true stories that prove I'm the right coach for you.

A CHANGE IN COURSE

> "You cannot be wimpy out there on the dream-seeking trail. Dare to break through barriers, to find your own path."
>
> – Les Brown

When I was 22, my aunt said to me: "You're not going to make it. You're Asian. There aren't many people on TV who look like you." I let that sink in, and it shook me to my core.

She said this to me at a time when my head was filled with self-doubt and my heart was filled with a dream of becoming a reporter and news anchor. I love my aunt. She isn't a distant relative that I would briefly rub shoulders with once a year at a family reunion. This aunt bought me new clothes and school supplies every fall when my family couldn't afford them. This aunt made me meals when my mom was working. Her opinion has always mattered to me.

My aunt is a strong, single, independent woman, and while she never had any biological children she helped raise me as her own. Growing up dirt poor in a family of 12, she often preached that a good education was the best way to get a good-paying job and a comfortable life. She's living proof that this approach works. She excelled in school in Singapore, and when she immigrated to Canada she secured a stable and successful career as a chartered accountant. I couldn't blame her or hate her for what she said. Her words stemmed from her experience and a genuine concern for my future. But I knew deep down that if I let her opinion stop me in my tracks before giving it my all, my dreams would never take flight.

Truthfully, she had a good point. There were only a small handful of news anchors and reporters who were people of colour on Canadian television in 2007. None of those I saw were Chinese. "You're not going to make it. You're Asian." Those words looped in my head and pushed me to be the best I could be. I so badly wanted to prove her wrong, and more importantly, to prove to myself it was possible.

Someone who gave me hope that my far-fetched dreams were possible was Connie Chung. I grew up watching the legendary Chinese American journalist, who has been an anchor and reporter for many major US television news networks.

Our family's living room TV has always had Canadian and American news playing because my mom loves to stay on top of what's going on in the world. Chung isn't Canadian, but that mattered less to me than the fact that she was one of the few people who looked like me in the media. While there are many women working in television news now, back in the '70s when Chung started her career, it was a different story. The added challenge of being someone of colour working in the spotlight made her work and what she accomplished even more impressive. She broke barriers and helped pave the way for me and those who follow in her footsteps.

"Rejection is merely a redirection;
a course correction to your destiny."
– Bryant H. McGill

When you know what you want to do with your life, the steps you need to achieve your goal become clearer. If that's you, BRAVO! You're one of the lucky ones. For most of us, discovering our life's purpose takes us on a winding road, filled with obstacles, objections, and distractions. Some of us have multiple purposes and passions at different points in our lives. My journey is a prime example.

At this point you know I had dreams of becoming a broadcaster when I was younger, but I need to rewind my story a few years to show you that it wasn't carved in stone. The earlier part of my journey is important because it shows:

Sometimes you have to lose yourself before finding the person you're meant to be.

When I was 17 and a senior in high school, I asked the school's academic counsellor for help with applying for university scholarships. I didn't want to ask my parents to help me pay for school. They were already under a lot of financial strain. They had recently filed for bankruptcy after their hobby fish shop went belly up (pun intended).

The counsellor asked me what I wanted to be when I grew up. I said I wanted to be a journalist. She responded, "Don't waste your time and talent on becoming a journalist. You should be a doctor." While I was disappointed that she didn't see me as a journalist, I could see her point. "Maybe she's right", I thought. "I'm always on the honour roll, I love science, and I enjoy volunteering to help people."

To the counsellor, medicine was a more promising career choice. As the daughter of working-class immigrants, I knew that becoming a doctor would produce prestige and financial stability for my family. After speaking with my Asian friends, it turns out *a lot* of our parents wanted us to become doctors, dentists, lawyers, and engineers. Some of my Asian friends wanted more than anything to follow a career path that would make their parents proud, but questions popped into my head: Is it my dream to become a doctor? Could I make it my dream? Do I even have what it takes to become a doctor?

I contemplated my whole life in front of me when I was 17. "What am I going to do with my life?" That's such a tough question. I didn't even know what I was going to do on the weekend! I worked hard to find a way to pay for my education. My prayers were answered. I was awarded several scholarships, which paid for my undergraduate degree in Communications in full.

While finances were figured out, I still felt my future was in limbo. I decided to keep my options open by taking both communications and science courses and because I wanted to graduate in four years, I took extra classes in the spring and summer.

The heaviness of what I *should* be doing with my life was weighing on me. I started to crack under the pressure while working on getting the Communications degree at the University of Calgary. I lived with a deep panic in my chest. It was hard to breathe whenever I thought about what career direction to take. I couldn't figure out what I wanted to do with my life. My inner voice kept asking "What will make me happy and also make my parents proud?"

Fast forward three years, and outwardly I looked like I was holding it all together. But inside, my outlook was hanging on by a thread. I fell apart during a session with an academic counsellor. She expected to chat about my career goals to help me decide my major, but what she got was an emotional meltdown. Fat tears rolled down my cheeks as we discussed the immense pressure I put on myself to meet internal and external expectations. She wasn't a trained therapist, but at that moment she acted like one and I'm grateful that she did. I loved science and serving others. Going for a career in medicine seemed like the right thing to do. After that meeting, I switched my major in my final year of university from Communications to Biological Sciences and graduated with distinction.

The next logical step was to take the Medical College Admission Test. Then I applied to different medical schools in Canada and waited for responses. All were rejections, except for one. I remember the day I received mail from the University of Alberta's medical school in Edmonton.

I ripped open the envelope and pulled out the letter. I gasped – I had gotten an interview! But instead of joy and excitement – a question popped into my head: "What if I never get to try broadcast journalism?"

That innocent thought was an earthquake moment that sent aftershocks through my life and what I wanted to do with it. Just days before my interview, I completely lost my voice because of a cold. The laryngitis was so severe, I could barely make out a few words before I went into a violent coughing fit. But I was told that if I didn't attend my interview, I would lose my spot. So I went, sick and virtually voiceless. Instead of the expected three interviewers, only two showed up for my interview. I answered the questions the best I could. I didn't feel like myself. I was filled with doubt about being accepted. I walked out of the interview unsure about my performance *and* my future.

What I *was* sure about was that I loved working in television and telling stories using video. Starting in my first year of university, I volunteered at NUTV, also known as New University Television, one of the oldest university-based television production societies in Canada. Working alongside other volunteers and learning from experienced storytellers, I helped to produce a community show capturing campus stories. I hosted a handful of episodes and reported and produced some stories. Although I loved it, I couldn't shake the thought that a career in medicine seemed more secure and I wanted to make my parents proud.

While applying for medical school, a friend had convinced me to apply to the Southern Alberta Institute of Technology (SAIT) Radio Television Broadcast News program. I applied last-minute as a backup plan just in case I didn't get into medical school. When I say last-minute, I *really* mean last-minute.

The clock was ticking, and my heart was racing as I bolted towards the SAIT program office on the last day applications would be accepted. I handed my application package to the receptionist and breathlessly asked "Did I make it?"

She glanced at the clock hanging on the wall: "You just made it – with two minutes to spare."

"HOLY MOTHER OF PEARL! That was close!" I blurted.

At the time I applied for the broadcast news program, spots were limited and those applying had to go through an interview process to secure one. It didn't faze me. I knew I had a good shot at getting in because of my volunteer experience creating video content. My intuition was correct. I was invited for an interview!

My health was back. This time, my voice stuck around – and so did my confidence. My volunteer experience hosting shows and producing videos helped me to answer every question the panel of judges threw my way. I knew in my gut that I nailed it. I walked out of that interview feeling like I could take on the world!

Maybe the laryngitis was part of divine intervention, or maybe it was unconscious self-sabotage. But I didn't get into medical school. Discouraged, I clung onto hope that my backup plan would work out. My parents were disappointed.

My dad said something to my mom that I'll never forget – *"How come no one wants our daughter?"*

I didn't hear him say it with my own ears. My dad and I rarely talked about anything personal. When my mom shared it with me, I worried I had let my parents down.

Even though I've always known they both love me, I can count on one hand how many times my parents have verbally told me that they're proud of me.

Maybe it's a cultural thing and the way both of them were brought up. Maybe that's why I have a relentless work ethic to succeed and earn the praise I want from them. Maybe that's why I felt lost and unwanted for months – until I opened up a letter from SAIT. I mouthed the words as I read them – "Congratulations Felicia. You have been accepted . . ."

ACCEPTED! Holy smokes! That single word lifted the cloud of confusion and snatched me out of the limbo I had been lost in for years. My heart was light and happy. My feet were happy, and I started dancing around the house and hollering "I got into the broadcast news program!"

Someone did want me!

I finally had a chance to answer my own question and try broadcast journalism! My rejection from medical school was actually a *redirection* that led me down the path of who I was meant to become.

Looking back, being a doctor wasn't my true calling. Sometimes things happen for a reason. A rejection is not the end of the world. It may mean "No forever" or it may mean "No, not right now." I'm eternally grateful for getting that big "NO." When rejection happens, dust yourself off and get back up again because:

A denial doesn't equal defeat.
Use a denial to give yourself space to pause, refocus, and drive you towards your destiny.

Video storytelling has become my vehicle to make a mark on the world. One of my favourite parts of being a journalist was helping the people I interviewed.

Now as a videography business owner, I mostly work with women entrepreneurs and people of colour.

As a content creator, I share tons of valuable tips to help people create videos with confidence. As Connie Chung inspired me to take risks and follow my dreams, I hope that my work helps to break barriers for those who follow me. It's my mission to help normalize the media landscape, so that who we see on our screens reflects who we see around us in our lives.

We need more voices and faces added to mix to create a kinder world. I want my daughters to grow up in a world where they see people like themselves and know they're worthy, valuable, and vibrant just the way they are. We're getting there, but there is still much work to be done. The internet has become the great equalizer. You no longer need to wait for someone to open the door for you. Figure out what you need to do to build the door yourself! When you rely on someone else's approval to make your dreams come true, you could be waiting forever, and be sorely disappointed in the process. The world is waiting to hear from you. I'm here to help empower you with the video and presentation skills you need to share your magic with the world – so you don't stay a secret any longer.

You don't need to read this book in a certain order, but a great deal of thought has gone into how it has been organized. In Chapter 1: P.R.E.P. for Success you'll build a strong foundation for the rest of the book by learning how to shoot and edit video properly. Chapter 2: Bring Out the Best You covers how you can start loving the way you look and sound on camera, including vocal warmups to improve the voice that you already have.

In Chapter 3: How to Set Yourself Apart from Everyone Else you'll learn about a powerful way to tell your own story and how to share your personal experiences for maximum impact.

Chapter 4: Your Stories in Your Style covers different video styles to help you find one that works best for you. If you want to learn how to be a more effective communicator when you host online talks or workshops, I highly recommend reading Chapter 5: How to Light Up a Room. I share my best wardrobe, makeup and hair tips to help you put your best face forward in Chapter 6: Camera-Ready Secrets. If the thought of negative feedback stops you from sharing your videos, head to Chapter 7: Overcoming Criticism and Crickets for some encouragement. Finally, in Chapter 8: You Are the Real Deal I help you tackle imposter syndrome so that you can drop the doubt and show up as the once-in-a-lifetime miracle that you truly are!

While the teachings and principles of this book are universal, much of this book has been written with love – for the grown women, and girls growing up, who don't feel like they are pretty enough, skinny enough, smart enough, special enough, old enough, young enough, or simply good enough to sit at the table. I've been called all but one of these things. I know how hard it is to believe in yourself when others don't. I want you to know you're not alone. I want you to know that you are enough, just as you are. And if this connects with you – from my heart to yours – I invite you to come sit at the table with me.

I genuinely want you to succeed at video creation and video confidence.

Valuable resources such as video tutorials and checklists have been made to complement this book to boost your knowledge and turn you into a video-making rock star!

Go to reelawesome.com/dontstayasecret to access them.

Chapter 1
P.R.E.P. FOR SUCCESS

"Get the fundamentals down and the level of everything you do will rise."
– Michael Jordan

"Come on. Work. WORK DAMN IT! ARGH!"

Silence.

"Is this all you got for me? Nothing. Nothing, after I spent the last hour heating you up!"

Talking to my camera got me nowhere. All I got from it was the "cold shoulder." Mother Nature held her icy grip over everything around me. My fingers throbbed under my gloves while I stepped out of my idling vehicle for a few minutes, only to dart inside the front passenger side for some reprieve and warmth. Breathing in the frigid air felt like inhaling a lit match. Snow blanketed the highways leading to my stop, and camouflaged patches of black ice. Thank God I made it to the site of the crash okay.

As my swollen fingers were soothed by the heat coming from the vehicle's vents, I glanced at the dashboard. Minus 42 degrees Celsius without the windchill. Brrr. Peering out the window, the only signs left of the serious accident were small fragments of scrap metal and serpentine tread marks that packed down the powder.

My assignment was to get footage of what was left of the accident to show the story for the evening news. The problem: my camera wasn't cooperating. My gear had been tucked securely in my camera bag at the back of the vehicle during the one-hour commute – just long enough to put it in a cold-induced coma.

"SNAP OUT OF IT!" I growled at the camera. It probably cost $50,000 brand new, but it wasn't pulling its weight in this situation. Hot air blew at full blast out of the vents against the machine as I tried again and again to revive it. Time was running out. The producers of the evening news in Regina would be expecting footage of the crash. I would need enough time to feed the video into the station. Rubbing my forehead, I nibbled on my lip until the solution came to me – the phone! It's not what we usually use to gather news, but it'll have to do, and right now it's the only way this is going to work.

Pulling out my work flip phone, I switched the camera to video mode and started rolling, capturing various angles of the scene. Once I was satisfied with my shots, I put the phone back in my purse and raced back to headquarters. I quickly pieced together the footage of the accident to match the script I wrote and transferred the video. Done! We should use our phones more often. After sharing the camera problems I had faced with the show's producers, they praised me for being resourceful. The flip phone wasn't worth $50,000, but it did the job that its more expensive counterpart couldn't when it really counted.

I'm here to deliver really good news! Chances are you have all the video production gear you need to start producing high-quality video. Another bonus?

It's so compact that it fits in the palm of your hand. It likely records in high-definition, if not better. If you've guessed that all hints are pointing to your smartphone, ding, ding, ding, you're correct! Your prize is the techniques and the lessons I'm going to teach you to create professional-looking videos with what you already have, and what you have is a gift compared to the flip phone I used to use.

Once on a video call with my mom, I pulled up my leggings to reveal a purple bruise about the size of my head that had taken over my thigh. She burst into tears, "Quit! It's not worth it!"

Stunned by her emotional response because, unlike me, my mom is not a crier, I tried to downplay what happened, "It's fine Mommy. It's just from my camera."

My bulky over-the-shoulder news camera hung on a crossbody strap and became a tenderizer, pounding my flesh every time I took a step as I moved from location to location. My fellow videographers once weighed the industry-level equipment we carried on our shoulders and around our waists. The camera, tripod, accessory bag filled with microphones, batteries and lighting equipment tipped the scale at roughly 50 pounds – 50 freaking pounds was about half my weight! No wonder it was hurting me. Professional videographers getting injured on the job and going on disability leave is not uncommon. The beauty of using your phone is that it's likely not going to create a massive bruise on your thigh, and it shouldn't cause you to throw out your back or pull your shoulder. Hallelujah! When you've had to carry heavy equipment, you're very thankful for production gear as light as your phone.

The idea that you need to buy expensive equipment to start making videos that matter is a misconception – it actually may be an excuse that's got your foot on the brakes. Let go of that thought about the need for expensive equipment, because if your phone can shoot video in at least HD quality, you have permission to move your foot to the gas pedal. Let me help save your hard-earned money by showing you what really works.

Creating engaging video isn't about the hardware. It's about how well you can use it to tell a story or share a message.

With the right tools, you can film professional-looking videos without breaking the bank. I'm a big believer that you should use what you already have.

All you need to own for a basic video production kit is the following:

1. Recording video and audio – A smartphone
2. Lighting – Access to natural light
3. Camera stabilizer – Anything that props up your phone at eye level, including using your hand to hold it

Once you're ready to invest more in your equipment, there are a few items that I recommend purchasing. If you're a one-person crew like me, it's helpful to have lightweight and portable equipment.

Here's what's in my upgraded video production kit:

1. Recording video – A smartphone
2. Recording audio – A microphone
3. Lighting – A ring light or a studio lighting kit with a light diffuser
4. Camera stabilizer – A stand such as a tripod with a handle for improved control

If buying new equipment isn't in your budget, don't worry – you don't need it to make videos. And if learning to use more gear is overwhelming, keep it simple and stick to using only your phone.

P.R.E.P. FOR SUCCESS

Impactful stories don't often magically come together. It can feel overwhelming and confusing to figure out the steps when creating video. That's why I created my signature P.R.E.P. for Success method, which takes you step-by-step from the planning stage to publishing and repurposing your content with confidence:

P is for **PLAN**
R is for **RECORD**
E is for **EDIT**
P is for **PUBLISH**

PLAN IS THE P IN P.R.E.P. FOR SUCCESS

Confidence comes with being prepared. Putting in the work before you edit the video will help make the whole process more enjoyable. There are five major aspects to keep in mind in the planning stage.

I'll take you through each of the levels of planning in the following order:

1. Lighting
2. Audio
3. Studio space
4. Video
5. Message

Lighting

Lighting is one of the most important parts of creating appealing videos. It can help set the mood and draw attention to the subject. Professional studio photographers often use oversized soft box studio lights and the images they capture make it easy to see why.

The bigger the light source, the more flattering the light. The biggest light source in the world is our sun. Shooting by a window is a great choice, and it doesn't cost anything! Take advantage of sunlight and shoot your videos during the day, with your face, or whatever you want to record, facing a window.

Sometimes direct natural light from the sun can look harsh and create shadows on your face. This usually happens mid-day when the sun is directly above you.

An easy fix to avoid this harsh mid-day sunlight is to move completely into a shadow. In other words, shoot in the shade. You're less likely to squint when looking into the camera and you'll look more relaxed and approachable in your video. Or you can use a light diffuser such as a light reflector to bounce light on your face and watch those strong shadows disappear!

One simple and inexpensive option that you may already have at home is using a white piece of cardboard as a light reflector. When you're shooting outside, finding a shady spot to shoot may mean sacrificing a pretty background, but at least you'll look better – and remember, you're the star of the show!

Ring light

If you have the budget to invest in lighting equipment, I recommend using a ring light because it's easy to set up, it's portable and it's affordable. A ring light is my go-to light for creating quick social media videos. The way I see it is, if a ring light is good enough for influencers and beauty professionals, then it's good enough for me! The pros use them because they can soften lines and wrinkles. However, because the phone holder is attached to the ring light, it doesn't work for everyone.

Tabletop ring light (left) and
ring light with tripod stand (right)

Studio lighting kit

If you wear glasses, it can be hard to avoid the reflections that show up on your lenses from a ring light. Eye contact is important to make a connection with the viewer. If you're comfortable to show up on camera without your glasses, then problem solved! Another way to work around wearing specs is to find a separate stand for your phone and move the ring light around until you don't see its reflection in your glasses. An easier option for people who wear glasses is to buy a lighting kit with 1-2 lights on stands that can be positioned so that the face is lit without capturing the ring light's reflection. For this option, you may want to buy a mobile phone stand, such as a tripod with a phone holder so you won't have to hold your phone when recording.

Ring light reflection wearing glasses

Two-point lighting system wearing glasses

Using additional lighting gives you the flexibility to shoot in the evening and in dim environments. If you must shoot in the evening or in a dark space, and you don't have additional lighting equipment, use lamps that you already own to help brighten your shots.

Audio

How annoyed or frustrated do you feel when you're watching a video and you can't hear what the person is saying? It can be hard to understand the story when you can't hear what's going on. Thankfully the built-in audio recording quality on most newer smartphones is good and, seriously, it better be when you're shelling out a pretty penny for a smartphone! One way to improve the audio quality is to shoot in a quiet space, and it's free!

When you're ready to upgrade your audio equipment, there are a ton of microphone kits on the market to choose from. But not all of them are worth buying. In my experience, the best microphones have their own internal power source. These microphones usually rely on batteries, either internal batteries that are rechargeable or replaceable ones. After testing several microphones out, I've found that microphones that piggyback on a phone's power don't do a good job of amplifying the sound captured by the microphone.

Before you buy a microphone, do your research. Watch video reviews of microphones that you're interested in. Make sure the microphone you're considering is compatible with your phone model and figure out if you'll need to buy any adapters to make it work. After you buy a microphone (with a good return policy), test it out for yourself.

Record audio with your phone, and then record audio using the microphone with your phone. If the audio sounds better with the microphone, it's a good sign that you've made the right choice.

I'm going to do my best to keep audio equipment as simple as possible based on the types of videos that I've made that you might be thinking of doing too. The microphone descriptions are meant to get you started in searching for your ideal microphone. If you'd like to see the exact audio gear I use to produce my content, please go to **reelawesome.com/dontstayasecret.**

One-spot talk videos:

<u>Lavalier microphones</u> – Lavalier microphones are small, discreet microphones that you can clip to the top you're wearing. Because you don't have to hold the microphone, you can use your hands. A lavalier microphone can be directly connected to your phone, making it easy to connect and remove each time you use it.

The connecting cord that goes straight from the camera to the person talking can make it harder to move around. When using a lavalier microphone, thread the cord underneath your clothes to hide it from view because seeing the wire can be distracting to viewers.

Wired lavalier microphone

<u>Shotgun microphones</u> – Shotgun microphones are long, narrow microphones that look like the barrel of a shotgun. Shotgun microphones come in a variety of pickup patterns, which means they can differ in how sensitive they are to the area of audio they record.

Buying a shotgun microphone with a narrow pickup pattern focuses on recording the audio directly in front of the microphone while cancelling unwanted background noise. This is the kind of shotgun microphone you'll want to choose if the reason you're buying a microphone is to record yourself speaking. Meanwhile, a shotgun microphone with a wide pickup pattern will record a lot more background noise around the subject.

One benefit of using a shotgun microphone is that it can be mounted directly to the camera or placed nearby the camera, freeing up the use of your hands and removing the need to hide any cords.

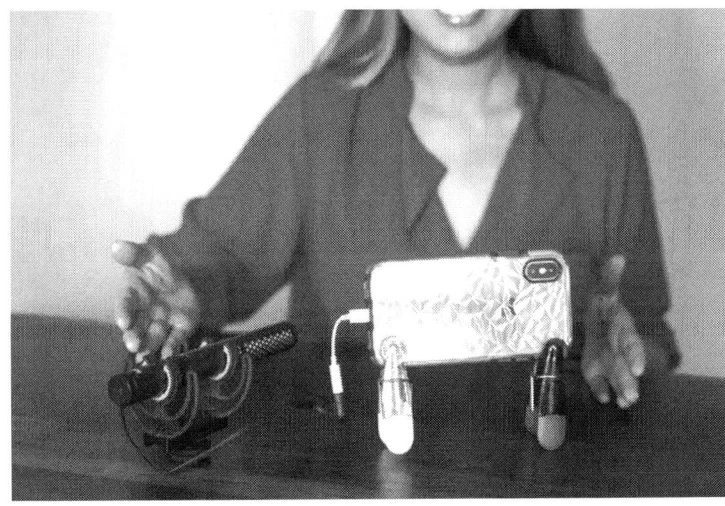

Shotgun microphone

Demonstration videos:

Wireless microphone systems – If you're moving around in your videos and you don't want to deal with being restricted by a cord, a wireless microphone system may be the right fit for you.

The wireless microphone system has two main parts: a transmitter and a receiver. The speaker wears the transmitter that captures the audio and relays it wirelessly to a receiver that's attached to the camera.

Many wireless microphone systems are designed to work with a lavalier microphone plugged into the transmitter. The wireless microphone system with a lavalier microphone allows the speaker to move freely because there's no cord between the speaker and the camera.

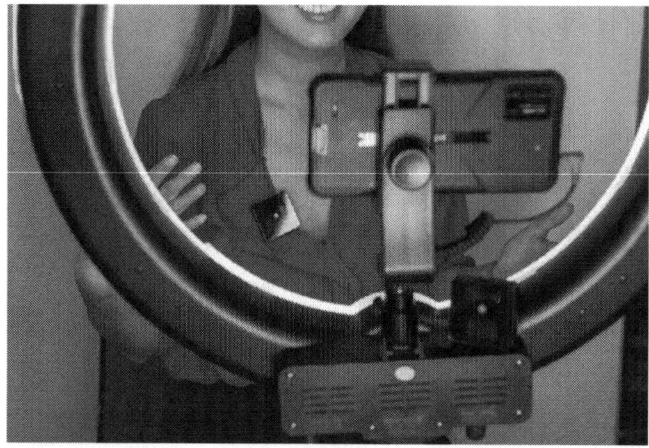

Wireless microphone system

Wireless microphone system with lavalier microphone

Podcasting and voiceovers:

Podcast microphones are designed to enhance the sound of your voice with studio-quality recordings. These microphones are usually meant to be set up in one spot, such as a desk. A USB microphone is popular for recording podcasts and voiceovers because it plugs right into a computer's USB port, simplifying the recording process. You'll need the right adapter if you use a USB microphone to record with your phone.

Podcast microphone

It's a good idea to use headphones or earphones to monitor the quality of the audio while you're recording, but it's not always possible because the port for the microphone can be the same one that you'd plug your headphones or earphones into. If this is the case, another way to monitor the audio is to perform a quick check after a test recording.

Once you've recorded several videos with your microphone and you're happy with the results, you can trust that it'll work well for you and monitoring your audio each time you record will become less important.

Studio space

Think of a video studio as the place where you capture your content. It can be one dedicated spot in your home, or several locations around your place. It can be a professional studio that you pay to rent. It can be your office. Your studio can be outside in your garden, or at your favourite ice cream shop where you're shooting for the day. The bottom line is that your studio doesn't have to be picture-perfect or pricey, but it should add to your overall message and not detract from it.

An ideal studio location:

- Is easily accessible
- Is easy to tidy up before a shoot
- Relates to your message or your brand when possible
- Is quiet, or the background noise can be controlled
- Has access to good lighting

Unless you're working on a special production that needs a specific location, choosing a location that's readily available whenever you're able to shoot will help encourage you to create more videos. By producing videos in your own studio, you'll be able to maximize efficiency and minimize costs. Using a place that's easily accessible helps cut down on the setup and teardown time. You'll spend less time travelling and can use that saved time to do other important tasks.

For example, you can designate a spot in your living room or office to shoot videos. You don't have to show the entire room; focusing on a corner that's easy to clean is fine.

I shoot in several locations around my home. With little kids there's plenty of clutter and toys around my place, so choosing specific areas that are easy to clear up before I hit record makes it easy for me to create more content. When I first became a mom, cleaning up a space in my cramped apartment before shooting DIY videos ate up a lot of time that I could have spent creating more content. It's important to keep the background of your videos tidy because first impressions matter. For example, a video with clothes piled up on the floor behind a professional organizer wouldn't convey professionalism or the person's ability to be organized. A new or returning viewer may think twice about hiring that professional organizer.

Deciding on how to style your studio is based on personal preference and budget. If you want to elevate your studio space, you can incorporate your brand colors or add a logo that's visible in the background. Think creatively and use what's available to you. Remember, your message matters more than your backdrop. Take it a step further and you could add some plants, pretty décor, or colourful backlighting – it's up to you.

Editing audio can be tricky. Imagine you're outside, recording a video of yourself speaking, and just when you feel like you're on a roll the sound of a motorcycle's engine revving butts in. Oh no! You may have to record again. If you're shooting indoors, be aware that microphones can pick up the change in noise coming from machines such as furnaces or air conditioners when they turn off and on.

Choose a studio location where the background audio won't be much of an issue or be prepared to record extra takes when something unexpected happens.

Sometimes shooting at a remote location makes more sense than shooting in your regular studio. For example, a food vlogger visiting Nova Scotia could use one or more of the Annapolis Valley's stunning vineyards to showcase the local food and wine in the area. A vlogger is someone who creates videos and posts them to a video blog. When there's an opportunity to take your viewers on a special experience with you, take advantage of it.

Video

When we're starting out with mobile video production, we'll use our smartphone to capture footage. You're welcome to upgrade once you have the means to buy a more expensive camera, and once you feel confident in creating videos with your phone. For now, everything I teach you will be about using your smartphone.

Video angles:

The angle you shoot your videos with has a big impact on how you look. It also influences the way you are perceived by your viewer. There are three main angle options: high, low and eye level.

High – High angle involves raising the camera slightly higher than your eye level so that you're shooting downwards towards your face. It adds definition to your features and can make you look slimmer.

However, if your lens is extremely high compared to your eyes, it will give a sense of smallness and vulnerability, much like a child does looking up to a parent.

Low – Shooting with a low angle makes you look more dominant and powerful. However, when you're shooting up towards your face, it also accentuates a double chin. If that's not what you're aiming for, shoot at a high level or at eye level.

Eye level – Shooting at eye level is simply what it sounds like. The point of view is set at your eye level. Recording videos at eye level is another excellent option because it puts your viewers at the same level as you and makes your viewer feel like they're right there with you.

High angle (left), low angle (middle), and eye level (right)

Nine steps to set up your smartphone for video success:

Now that we've gone over lighting, audio quality, and setting up your studio space, you're ready to set up your phone to start shooting great-looking videos. Here's a quick start guide to set up your phone so you can hit the ground running with sharp video for whatever platform you decide to use.

I've written this book for both Android and Apple phone users, so you won't find detailed step-by-step instructions in this chapter for specific phones. If you'd like to watch a tutorial to that covers this step-by-step checklist, go to **reelawesome.com/dontstayasecret.**

1. **Make space for video** – Clear unwanted items off your phone so there's enough space to store your video files. Video eats up a lot more storage than photos, so be prepared to make room on your phone for all the videos you're going to create. You can save them on another device such as your desktop computer, an external hard drive or on digital storage platforms such as Google Drive or on a video platform such as YouTube. It's important to stay on top of maintaining the storage space on your phone so you won't run into the issue of having to delete files in the middle of a new shoot to free up space. You may need to go to the deleted file folder on your phone to clear all the unwanted items and free up storage space.
2. **Decide on the video resolution** – If publishing clear and sharp videos is important to you, make sure your camera is set to record in the highest image quality your phone will allow. This is especially important because some social media platforms compress videos. By recording in the highest resolution your phone will give you, even when your videos are downgraded, they'll still appear sharper than if you recorded them with a lower resolution. The biggest drawback is these high-resolution video files will take up more space on your phone.

   For example, I intentionally shoot videos in 4K Ultra High-Definition (UHD) resolution instead of 1080p Full High-Definition (FHD). One of the main differences between 1080p and 4K video is image quality.

There are almost four times the number of pixels captured in 4K video compared to 1080p video; this big difference leads to sharper videos with greater fine detail. As technology advances and shooting in 8K or greater become default options, recording videos at the highest image quality available on your phone will allow your content to look better in the long run.

Frame rate refers to the how many images are captured one after another in one second and is measured in frames per second (fps). Common frame rates that you can record videos in include 30 fps and 60 fps. Shooting at 60 fps creates smoother-looking videos than at 30 fps. However, a video recorded at 60 fps is larger than one recorded at 30 fps.

For most of the videos you'll create using this book, I recommend shooting in 4K UHD at 30 fps when possible.

3. **Wipe your lenses** – Imagine this: you have your camera set to record at its highest quality, but the screen shows everything looks fuzzy. Try cleaning the lenses. Use a soft cloth, rather than a tissue because that can leave tiny fibres behind, and wipe away possible smudges and fingerprints. It's good practice to clean both the front and back lenses so you'll be ready to capture footage with both lenses.
4. **Decide on the video orientation before you shoot** – It's much easier to edit a video if you shoot a video in one orientation compared to if you switched in the middle of recording. Long-form videos are generally shot in a horizontal or landscape orientation.

Short-form videos are usually recorded in a vertical or portrait orientation. However, this isn't a hard and fast rule; many social media platforms allow you to post videos recorded in either orientation. Pick an orientation before you shoot and please don't overthink it. If you want to repurpose your long-form video onto a platform that favours vertical video, editing apps allow you to crop your video into a vertical video.

5. **Stabilize your smartphone** – I highly recommend investing in a tripod with a cellphone holder to shoot your videos. It's not necessary, but it will greatly improve the quality of your videos. Unless it's done intentionally, shaky videos look amateur. If you don't have a tripod yet, you can prop your phone up against an object so that it's about eye level when you record your videos.
6. **Hook up a microphone** – If you don't have a microphone yet, don't sweat it! This step is optional. You can still create engaging videos by using your phone's built-in microphone.
7. **Frame it right** – Proper framing will help your videos look professional. You can adjust your camera angle during this step. A useful tip is to turn on the grid feature in your phone's settings. Once you have gridlines on your screen, frame yourself in the centre of the screen when you shoot a video of yourself.

   Professional videographers and photographers generally use the Rule of Thirds to achieve proper framing. The best place for your subject is where the lines intersect.

When you've framed up a shot that includes a person's head and shoulders, the person's eyes should be two-thirds of the way up, which falls on the upper grid line.

Framing a subject with gridlines

8. **Lock the exposure and focus** – This is especially important when you're shooting a video where the lighting and movement changes quickly. Each time you open your camera on your phone to shoot, it starts off in auto-exposure and autofocus mode. The auto-exposure adjusts the brightness of the image and the autofocus adjusts its sharpness.

You can access this feature on most Apple and Android phones by touching what you want in focus, and then holding down on the screen for a couple of seconds. This should lock the camera's focus and exposure to what you see at that moment on your screen.

So, when light drastically changes around you, it will continue to keep those settings and you won't unexpectedly look brighter and then darker in your video and you should stay in focus.

Locking the exposure and focus on an Android phone

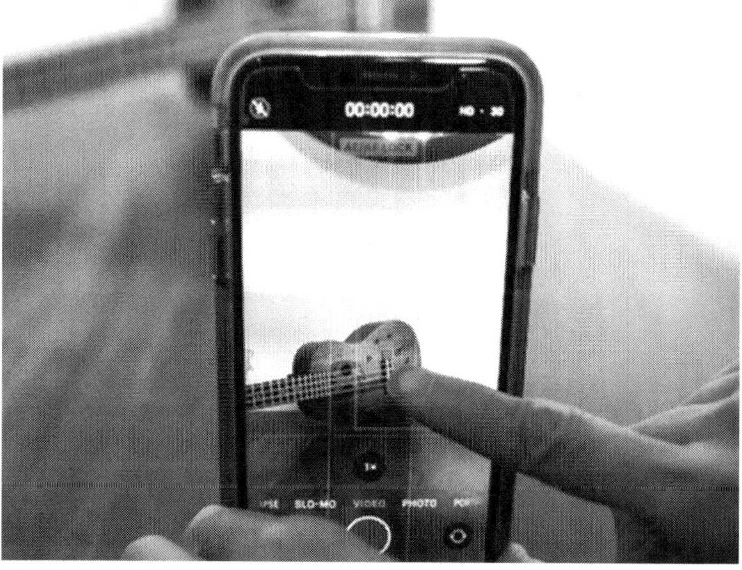

Locking the exposure and focus on an Apple phone

9. **Do a visual check** – You may find it easier to shoot using the front camera, which is the same camera you use to take selfies. Take advantage of using this camera by checking how your background looks. Make sure that nothing strange is poking out of the back of your head on the screen. It will save you from having to reshoot later. It's also a good idea at this stage to check if you have anything in between your teeth.

   If you use the rear camera to shoot your videos, you'll have to do a visual check after recording your videos.

Nine steps may seem like a lot to run through when you make a video, but going through each of them is more important at the beginning of your video-making journey so you start with a strong foundation. Once you're comfortable creating videos, it'll become second nature and you'll figure out which steps you need to repeat and the ones you can skip each time you create a new video.

Other video features:

Your smartphone has a lot of cool image-altering features. But all the options can get overwhelming. There are a few features in particular that you may find useful creating videos:

1. **Zoom** – Most phones can zoom into what you're seeing on your screen. The downside is using the zoom function can create a distorted image. When possible, zoom in by physically moving closer to what you want to shoot.

Before using the zoom feature on an Apple phone

After using the zoom (2x) feature on an Apple phone

2. **Slow motion and time lapse** – Slow motion captures video at a high frame rate, so when it's played back the action recorded looks smooth even when it's slowed down. Using slow motion video works well when you want to emphasize action.

   When you want to speed up action recorded over a long time, use the time-lapse feature. With time-lapse video, the frame rate is stretched out, so when it's played back, the action over time appears sped up.

Message

Planning is important to create an effective message. It takes time to do this, but it's worth the investment. I've found that a useful way to plan the message of a video is to think of it as the way you eat an ice cream cone that's made up of three main parts:

1. Opening
2. Body
3. Closing

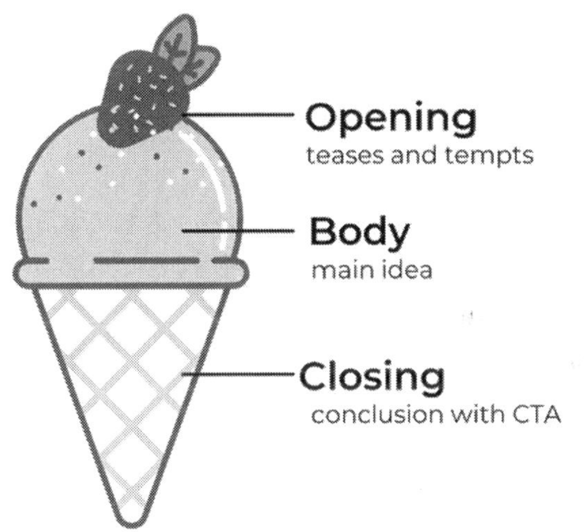

Opening:

You only have a few seconds to convince people to keep watching your video, so grab their attention fast! Imagine building the message of your video in the way you eat an ice cream cone, from the top down.

Start with the eye-catching toppings, such as sprinkles, and fruit to boot (fancy ice cream lovers unite!). Toppings add excitement, and draw a person in, and that's what the opening of your video does.

The toppings serve to tempt and tease the viewer. A decked-out ice cream cone will make you want to gobble it up. When you start your video off with a bang, it has a similar effect – the viewer will stick around a little longer.

There are different ways to create a compelling opening. If you're solely speaking on camera in your video, your hook could be asking a question to engage, telling a compelling fact, or telling a tasteful joke that your audience can relate to.

Body:

The body of your message is much like the ice cream itself. It contains the main idea of your video and all the delectable details. When planning the body of your message, ditch the word-for-word script. Instead, write your message in point form using an outline. Keep it simple, 1-3 points is usually the right amount of information to include in a single video. It's easier to be confident on camera when you have fewer things to remember.

Pro tip: Tape a piece of paper with your outline close to the camera lens in case you need to quickly refer to it when you're recording.

Closing:

The closing, like the cone comes last. Tossing that crispy wafer would be a waste. The same goes for the closing. The end of your message is important. Get your viewers to take action and tell them exactly what you want them to do.

It could be building awareness about who you are, or it could be to drive signups to a program you have. This is known as the Call To Action (CTA).

Pro tip: Adding the word FREE to your CTA is a non-threatening way to encourage your viewers to take action.

These are some examples of Calls To Action:

- Reach out to me if you have questions
- Subscribe
- Tap on the share button
- Tag a friend who could really benefit from this
- Book a free discovery call
- Get a free quote
- Get instant access to this free gift worth $100
- Signup for email updates

It's nice to make content with no strings attached occasionally, but think of it this way – if you do all the work to create the content, without asking someone to save it or share it or buy your product, then you're missing out on engagement – and missing out on boosting your bank account.

Teleprompter:

As a professional news reader, I sat behind an anchor desk for more than seven years and read scripts off a teleprompter every day. Tripping up on a word when you're on a live broadcast can be embarrassing. I usually wrote my own scripts when I was anchoring, but one time when I was delivering a late-night newscast, I wasn't able to review a sports script that a producer wrote before I delivered it on the air.

As I was reading each word, an unfamiliar one popped up – "BEAUSEJOUR" – my hands gripped the edge of the anchor desk tightly as I scrambled to find the answer, "What's that word? How on earth do I say that?" My noisy brain connected with my mouth, but it spat out "BOURGEOISIE" instead. Oh no! My cheeks flushed, and I stumbled through the rest of the script. I was unprepared, and it didn't help that I couldn't read or speak French. What I learned is that a teleprompter is there to prompt you, but you still need to know what you're saying and how to say it ahead of when you deliver it.

When you avoid scripting every word, you'll be less likely to trip over what you say and come off as more approachable and natural. While I encourage you to memorize the points of your message, some of my clients have found using a teleprompter app on their phone gives them an added level of comfort with presenting. If you decide to use a teleprompter program on your phone, make sure the words are close to the lens, and rehearse plenty of times to boost confidence in what you're saying, so it comes out naturally and doesn't look or sound like you're reading.

RECORD IS THE R IN P.R.E.P. FOR SUCCESS

You'll find useful tips and strategies on how to present with confidence on camera in the next chapter. One piece of advice I'll provide here is that if you're soft spoken, remember to speak up when you're recording so the microphone can pick up what you're saying more clearly. And after you record your video, don't forget to review it.

It gets easier the more you do it.

Please resist the urge to be perfect. When I was starting out as a video journalist in Saskatchewan, I was assigned to cover a parade. Capturing the interviews and footage was a piece of cake. Getting a 15-second clip of myself talking on camera, also known as a standup in TV broadcasting, was anything but. With no one else to check my framing and focus, I shot that standup at least fifteen times. The parade was almost over when I finally got everything the way I wanted it to look. What should have taken a few minutes to set up and record, took me an hour and a half because I wanted everything to be just right. I've wasted so much time trying to get the perfect take for the camera. So don't be a perfectionist when it comes to recording yourself.

Your first video won't be your last. Even if you improve by only 1% with each video you do, by the 100th video you will be 100% better than you were on your first try. But you won't need to create 100 videos to notice a huge improvement in the way you create your videos and the way you present yourself and your message.

When I started hosting TV shows more than two decades ago, it was easy to tell that I was a newbie. My first few videos are kind of embarrassing, and I can laugh at myself now because I've done a lot of work to get better and I didn't give up.

Capturing footage in addition to speaking clips helps tell a story. This is called "b-roll." While clips of someone speaking is considered primary footage, b-roll is secondary footage. You can add b-roll in with your primary footage to set the scene to help show what is happening in the scene and to make the video more interesting.

An effective way to capture b-roll is to shoot the same subject from different distances and you can get creative by capturing b-roll from different angles, such as from the ground and from high above.

If any of this is overwhelming, I'm here to help. You may find learning about shooting and editing video much easier with personalized coaching instead of reading about it. If so, email me at hello@reelawesome.com and write in the subject line: "Video coaching."

EDIT IS THE E IN P.R.E.P. FOR SUCCESS

The editing stage happens once you've gathered all the footage you're going to use, and the creativity doesn't stop once you're finished shooting. Video editing is an art and it can be really fun, especially once you get comfortable doing it. In this phase of the process you may sift through your clips, add graphics, and then layer on audio, such as a voiceover and music.

You don't have to shell out big bucks for the hardware and the software to edit slick videos. There are powerful mobile video editing apps that you can download for free. At the risk of sounding like a dinosaur, I started out recording and editing news stories on videotape. This was called tape-to-tape editing, or linear editing. Before videotapes were popular, film reels were physically cut into long strips, and then glued or taped back together to create a sequence that became the story. Video editing technology has come a long way! Now you can edit videos wherever you go.

A significant part of my life has been spent in dimly lit editing rooms, alone or sometimes with a professional editor, as I combed over clips and agonized over just the right sequence to illustrate a point while fine-tuning sounds to make a story come alive. There have been many moments when I've wanted to rip my hair out when an editing program crashed, and moments when a finished video moved me to tears. Over my career, I've used many different programs to edit news stories, business promo videos, short-form videos, and short documentaries. I'm going to save you time and headaches by teaching you some editing basics that you can use right away.

There are many desktop editing programs on the market, but we'll be sticking to mobile video editing because I want you to be able to create videos from start to finish using only your phone. There's no need to transfer files to your desktop and back to your phone before posting. I'm giving you a crash course on the basics of video editing. To find out my latest recommendations for editing apps and examples of how I use them, please check out **reelawesome.com/dontstayasecret.**

Important editing terms

- *Video clip* – Any short video that is less than the length of the video project that it's a part of is considered a video clip. Video clips are also simply called clips.
- *Timeline* – This chronological display allows the editor to lay out all the video and audio pieces of a project horizontally across the screen.

- *Cut* – A quick transition where one shot is instantly followed by another. Please note that if you're interested in learning how to cut sections out of a video, it won't be covered in this book.
  It's much easier to learn more advanced editing in a video or during a coaching session with me.
- *Trim* – Much like giving hair a trim, this action removes the beginning and/or the end of the clip. Please refer to the video exercise in this chapter, which will guide you to trimming a single video clip.

Editing is so important to the visual storytelling process because it can reflect the way we see the world and the way we want others to see it. Great editing takes all the pieces of the story and brings them together. The art of editing lies in the way we can evoke emotional response or get someone to take action.

Important editing principles

- *Get comfortable with the program* – While the tools and features may look different among video editing apps, the principles are the same. I've tested a lot of mobile video editing apps. Spend some time playing around with your editing program to become familiar with the tools you need to make awesome videos!
- *Create a story with your footage* – We are built to enjoy stories. Your video should include a beginning, middle and end. The video and audio elements that you choose to include should move the story along.

- *Start with your best material* – Use the most attention-grabbing material you have to start off your videos. It can be a clip of someone speaking (including yourself), your most captivating footage, or the best sound that accompanies video that you recorded. This strategy will help to draw your audience in at the beginning of your video.
- *Keep it interesting* – Unless you're editing a long-form informative video, such as an interview or documentary, move quickly between ideas, and shots. Attention spans are quite short, so if you linger on one point, without moving along to the next one, viewers are likely going to quit watching your video.
- *Use graphics with intention* – Animations, stickers, and lower-thirds (such as the name and title of a person), can make your video more engaging and informative. But go easy on the effects. Like adding salt to a meal – too much can be overpowering and unappetizing. Having a purpose for each of the graphics you use will make your life easier and it'll make it easier for your viewers to keep watching.
- *Take breaks* – It's easy to lose track of time when you're concentrating on editing. Remember to rest your eyes and walk away from the screen for your own mental health. Making editorial decisions can be difficult when you've been staring at a screen for a really long time.
- *Review and fine-tune* – Watch the project from the beginning to the end and keep an eye out for anything that has to be corrected before it's published.

VIDEO EXERCISE ON TRIMMING A VIDEO CLIP

It takes courage to put yourself out there in a video. This step-by-step exercise is designed to help you boost your confidence editing videos, so let's put all that video production knowledge you've just learned into practice!

Please record a short video of yourself answering these two questions:

1. What's the most interesting thing you've learned from this book so far?

____

____

____

2. What are you excited to achieve as your video confidence grows?

____

____

____

Before you begin to record, make sure you've run through the PLAN and RECORD sections of the P.R.E.P. for Success framework so you're starting off on the right foot.

Take a deep breath, smile, and hit record. You got this! It's okay if you try more than once to get it right, but please don't obsess over getting it perfect. Done is better than perfect.

Once you have one clip that you're happy with, stop. Now it's time to edit. You can trim this video in two ways: either by clicking on the video file itself where it's saved on your phone or by using a video editing app that you've downloaded.

If you're going to trim this video using what's already available on your Apple or Android phone, go to folder where the video is saved, select the video and hit the edit button which may look like an icon on some phone models.

If you decide to use an editing app that you downloaded, open a new project. Select the clip you're going to use for the video and add it to the timeline.

Next, for both methods, play the video. Is there dead air at the beginning? Let's remove it by trimming it. You should see thick vertical bars at both ends of the clip.

To trim the start of the clip, select the clip. Then hold down on the thick vertical bar at the beginning of the clip and drag it until you only include the part of the clip you want in the video. Watch it again.

Once you're happy with how it looks, clean up the end of the clip in the same way. Trim the excess at the back end of the clip by holding down on the thick vertical bar and move it to the point just after you finish speaking. Watch the whole video to make sure it's edited the way you like before you save it.

Hurrah! You just edited your first video with me! High-five!

I would love it if you posted this video online and tagged me on Instagram or TikTok @reelawesomeproductions, or submitted it directly to me at hello@reelawesome.com so that I can share it with my audience. Once you feel comfortable applying this editing assignment to other videos you make, you can move on to the next assignment.

If you need a visual demonstration of how to trim one clip, please check out **reelawesome.com/dontstayasecret** to watch the tutorial.

PUBLISH IS THE SECOND P IN P.R.E.P. FOR SUCCESS

Find the right fit for you and your audience

Don't give into the pressure of posting on every social media platform. Instead, focus on the right channels for your brand, and consider how much you can handle. If all you can handle is creating content for one specific social media platform, then focus on growing your presence on that platform. You can narrow down which platform will work best for you by doing market research to learn where your audience spends most of their time so you can forge meaningful connections and grow your brand. I started posting on YouTube first and then as I got more comfortable making content, I added Instagram and then TikTok to the mix.

Post consistently

A content calendar and scheduling strategy can save you time, stress, and keep you moving towards your marketing goals. Schedule posts at a rate that works for you. If you can't post five videos a week, and two is all you can do, then stick to that. You can always add more content when you're able to do it. By staying consistent with posting content, you'll build trust with your audience who will come to expect those two videos a week from you.

Hook them with a great headline

Before you publish your video, don't forget to jazz up the title that introduces it. Your video should deliver on what the title promises; otherwise you might lose viewers and followers. By crafting an eye-catching headline, you can capture the attention of users who are bombarded with a sea of social media clutter that grows every second.

Some tips for crafting an alluring title include:

- Replace "I" and "Me" to "You" and "Your" to put your audience's needs first (e.g., "Delicious plant-based food you need to add to your pantry")
- Use the word "This" to create immediacy and urge the viewer to click on the video (e.g., "Watch this if you want to create luxe wedding décor for less")
- Use numbers, facts and figures when appropriate because they're eye-catching (e.g., "The 10 best cleaning products on a budget")
- If you're writing a title for a tutorial, use the phrase, "How To" because it promises to teach your viewer something (e.g., "How to cook the fluffiest pancakes ever")

Repurposing Content

Make life easier for yourself and expand your reach to broader audiences by repurposing your videos on different social media platforms. It may seem like a lot of extra work, but it doesn't have to be. Repurposing a piece of content happens when you either change its format or present to a different audience by posting to another platform.

You can take short-form videos from one platform and repost them on another platform. For example, when this book was written a short TikTok video could be reused as an Instagram Reel and as a YouTube Shorts video. The same goes for long-form videos. An in-depth YouTube video could be used as an Instagram TV video. A long-form video could be edited into several short videos and posted onto platforms that are meant for short-form videos. Alternatively, you could combine several related short-form videos together to make a long-form video.

When you adopt the P.R.E.P. for Success method, you're following a solid blueprint that takes you from the planning stage to publishing your video content.

Technology advances at lightning speed. Social media trends evolve. The P.R.E.P. for Success method will help you create professional-looking videos despite these changes. You may not have gone to school for videography or work for a big production company, but armed with these tools you can be unstoppable. And once you have a solid foundation for producing videos, the next important step is to remove blocks that are stopping you from creating video content – and that's the focus of the next chapter.

Chapter 2
BRING OUT THE BEST YOU

"Be yourself; everyone else is already taken."
– Oscar Wilde

"Creating a custom statement hairpiece is...uh...uh...ugh. I can't remember what I'm supposed to say. Can I see the script again?"

"Felicia, this is the sixth time we've had to reshoot this clip. Come on. This is taking forever."

"Sorry Andrew. It's got to be just right. Thanks for being so patient."

Sighing, he tossed the script into my hands. "It doesn't have to be perfect. Just get it done. This isn't supposed to take all day."

But it was heading that way. It usually did. This time we were recording a how-to video about creating a custom floral hair comb on a budget. Whether it was a DIY craft, or an instructional food video, it always took longer than expected. A one-hour shoot often turned into three, or four, or sometimes five.

When I first started my YouTube channel, *Most Delightful Way*, I scripted each line that I would say for every video I created. We would record a new take each time I made a mistake. With my experience as a news anchor, I had an expectation that my delivery needed to be perfect.

While I had a hard time letting go of my perfectionism, Andrew was there to remind me that it's okay not to be perfect.

Andrew has stood by me – and by the camera – through it all. My husband is a gem. My friend once described Andrew as "Prince Charming." In many ways he is. He makes you feel valued and goes out of his way to be a good friend. Intelligent, funny, and handsome with a heart of gold, Andrew is a keeper. When I first started my YouTube channel, he helped with some of the shooting. He cleaned up baby toys and clutter from sections of our tiny apartment so we could have a tidy studio space to work with, while I fussed with curling my hair and blended three shades of eyeshadow to make my eyes pop. We would shoot tutorials together when our baby was napping, and I would shoot solo while he took her on adventures out of the home. The sheets on my side of the bed would often remain untouched as I'd glance up at the top of my desktop screen to take a break from editing – 1:04 am – another night, another time – 2:15 am. Producing content this way wasn't sustainable for our lifestyle, and we were both growing tired of it.

DON'T LET PERFECTIONISM BECOME YOUR MASTER

Perfectionism can be paralyzing. When it comes to video production, it slows the whole process down. I've lowered the bar when it comes to how much time I put into my hair and makeup since my early days as a digital content creator. But lowering the bar doesn't mean having no standards. The goal is to have realistic standards that fit your life.

Instead of taking an hour – yes, I'm embarrassed to admit I used to take a really long time to get ready for my DIY YouTube videos – I'm happy with how I look after ten minutes of getting camera-ready. Most of us don't have the luxury of a full team of makeup artists and stylists to help us look picture-perfect. Wanting to look your best is important, but trying to look perfect and polished each time you show up on camera can be time-consuming and a big barrier that stops you from wanting to shoot videos in the first place. Unless your business and message revolve around your appearance, putting in some effort is good enough. I share valuable tips on how to look your best on camera in Chapter 6: Camera-Ready Secrets.

Not only did I want to look polished in my videos, but I wanted to sound polished too. Writing scripts and reading off a teleprompter was a big part of my job as a news anchor. So, when I started my YouTube channel after leaving my career as a journalist, I still felt inclined to carefully script my videos. As my fan base grew, more viewers commented on my delivery, "You sound like a news reporter." While a part of me was proud that I sounded like a professional broadcaster, I was no longer a news anchor sharing serious stories about crime, natural disasters, and politics; I was now a digital content creator sharing original tutorials about such things as how to create wedding décor on a budget and easy baby shower decorations. It finally clicked: my perfectionism was getting in the way of being authentic in my videos. I had to stop being "Felicia the news anchor" and learn how to be me – the REAL ME – on screen.

Being real in my videos has meant being okay to show people that I'm not perfect (no surprise here, because I'm definitely not perfect).

After I started my videography business, I decided to stop scripting my videos word-for-word. Running a business, finishing client projects, and taking care of two little girls made time my most precious commodity. By creating outlines of what I wanted to cover, and delivering a few key points, I was able to produce many more videos in a shorter amount of time. Unless it was a major mess-up, I resisted reshooting clips of myself speaking, even when there were little mistakes. Knowing that I could publish a video with a small flub and nothing bad would happen has been liberating! The more videos I've created using the mindset that it's okay not to be perfect, the more I've been able to speak from my heart instead of speaking from a script. If this way of thinking helps you to make more videos, I encourage you to use it! People want to get to know the real you – flaws, flubs, and all!

Keep making videos and learn from each one you publish. Ask for feedback and be open to suggestions that could help make you and your videos better. I know the thought of making videos can be scary, but when you have a powerful message that needs to be shared, then pushing through perfectionism and doubt is worth it. Humans are smart. We can usually tell when someone isn't being true to themselves. When you have the courage to be yourself with others, that's when true connections are made.

REFLECTION EXERCISE ON PERFECTIONISM

Has anyone ever told you that your standards are too high? Do you have trouble letting other people do a task for you? Are you so overwhelmed by every task because you have to control every detail? Do you find yourself criticizing other people's work as well as your own work? Perfectionism is a highly inflexible way of focusing on small details of an activity to the detriment of getting that activity done. Perfectionism can cause conflict in relationships, issues at work, and getting work done – including making videos.

Learning to recognize perfectionism

If you're not a perfectionist, move on to the next section of this chapter. If you are one, or you're not quite sure if you have a problem with perfectionism, answer the following questions:

Do I usually feel depressed, angry, or frustrated while trying to meet my own standards?

Do my expectations of myself get in the way of finishing tasks or acting spontaneously?

Do I redo things over and over to improve them and still not feel satisfied?

Has perfectionism ever stopped me from getting something important done?

If you answered "YES" to any of these questions, perfectionism may be one of the reasons you're having issues making videos.

Ways to overcome perfectionism

- Think realistically. Nobody's perfect. We all make mistakes, which makes us human and relatable.
- Change your mindset around failure and rejection, because both are opportunities for growth.
- Step back and look at the big picture. Figure out if focusing on the details will help you get the task done. Ask yourself "What degree of imperfection can I live with?"
- Practice being imperfectly you. Let little mistakes go. Do one take of a video. Even if you make a mistake, challenge yourself to post it.
- Go easy on yourself. Getting used to more realistic standards involves time and practice.

Reward yourself

When you publish a video without having to reshoot it multiple times because you're fine with the imperfections, or posting the video after a quick edit, treat yourself! A reward can be spending time with loved ones, taking a walk, or trying a new restaurant. You deserve it!

There's nothing wrong with wanting things to look and feel great. Perfectionism can help you be successful and perform at a high level. But often when it comes to video, polished doesn't necessarily mean more views. Letting little mistakes get published makes you more human and relatable. Your audience can sense when you're raw and real and when you're being yourself. Video editing becomes simpler when you can live with minor mess-ups in your recordings. So don't sweat the small stuff.

When you get lost in the small details and let the fear of rejection and failure control your actions, trying to be perfect becomes a problem. When that happens remember

Don't let perfectionism become your master.

JUST STRUT

"To fall in love with yourself is the first secret to happiness."
– Robert Morley

"It's so good to see you!" My joy was palpable as I felt the strength in my grandaunt's arms as mine wrapped around her slender body. It had been years since our last hug. Her eyes scanned me from top to bottom.

"Felicia! Aiyo. What happened to you? You're so plump now. You need to go on a diet!" she announced in her operatic voice.

Nodding, I whispered, "I know."

After politely excusing myself from the reunion in front of our family-owned hobby fish shop, I turned the corner, slumped against the side of the brick building, and began to sob alone.

My love and respect for my grandaunt ran deep. Separated by miles and oceans, we spent more time apart than together. But whenever we were together, I quickly grew attached to her infectious charisma and kindness. A strikingly beautiful person, her lips were forever dressed in ruby red, and each strand of her inky black locks always seemed to be fixed in place. A God-praising woman, she was the kind of person I loved being around; but after her words cut me down, and I felt like I needed to be by myself.

My sleeve turned damp as I struggled to keep my cheeks dry. "Maybe I do need to go on a diet," I thought to myself. "That boy I didn't even know at school pointed at me and called me a fat Chinese girl." Cleaning off the salty specks that dried on my glasses, I tried to pick up the pieces of my shattered fragile ego. "I may not be pretty," I said to myself, "but at least I'm smart and kind". From that moment on, I've gone out of my way to be kind, to help others and to achieve academically. But my low self-esteem continued to follow me around like a lost puppy, mostly because of the way I saw myself.

Being a 12-year-old girl can be tough. It was for me. Hormones are in flux. My body morphed from thin to curvy, and baggy clothes helped to cloak my insecurities. I had to sort through mixed messages about food and body image. At family gatherings, older aunties encouraged my brothers and I to fill up on food, commanding, "Eat – EAT MORE!" Yet other times they'd comment on our weight: "You've gained weight" and "You used to be skinny. Now you're round."

OH MY SOUL! It was so confusing then, and it's still confusing, even when you're on the receiving end as an adult.

When I was in my early twenties, my relationship with a boyfriend ended on a sour note and I hit a low point. But it was the shakeup I needed to wake up. When my broadcast news classmate, Lisa Nguyen, found out what happened, she piped up: "Just strut! Work it, Felicia!"

After that, whenever I started feeling down about myself, I would say the words, "Just strut, just strut, JUST STRUT!" It instantly filled me with a sense of pride and power. "Just strut!" means to be unapologetically you, and to let the world know you're proud of the person staring back at you in the mirror!

I had enough of putting myself last. I was tired of my self-doubt and body-doubt. "JUST STRUT!" changed the way I looked at myself. This transformation didn't happen overnight. It took months of reminding myself that I was someone worth being proud of. I invested my time and energy improving my health and started celebrating my positive qualities, and because of that my confidence grew. At that point I was 23-years-old and, for the first time in my life, I really believed I was beautiful – inside and out.

I'm so grateful for the ongoing encouragement that Lisa gave me with those two powerful words. "JUST STRUT!" has continued to be a huge mantra for me and, if it feels right, Lisa and I want it to be yours too! Whenever you want to shake off feeling down about the way you look while channelling your inner star, remind yourself to "JUST STRUT!" Picture me right there with you as your hype-woman. I'll be cheering you on – "Work it! DAMN – you look good!"

I've given it a lot of careful thought and now I understand why my grandaunt's comment about my appearance when I was 12 affected me so much. Her words amplified the insecurities that I already had about myself. Although I never got the chance to ask her why she said what she did while she was alive, I know for sure that because of my grandaunt's loving character that she never meant to hurt me. She may have made those remarks because she was shocked at my weight gain and wanted me to live a healthier lifestyle. It's been more than two decades since then, and there are days where I still judge myself for what I do look like and what I don't look like. Much of my body still jiggles when I move. My lines aren't as fine anymore. But there's so much more to me than the number I see on the scale and the wrinkles on my face. Knowing my grandaunt didn't mean to hurt my feelings allowed me to forgive her. While that wound scarred me, forgiveness helped me to heal, move forward, and share my story from a place of wisdom and peace.

Learning to love yourself takes time and hard work. Take comfort that most of us are on our own self-love journey. Whenever you need a boost of self-confidence, pull your shoulders back, stand up tall, and get ready to:

Just strut.

REFLECTION EXERCISE ON RECOGNIZING YOUR OWN SCARS

At some point in your life, someone has said something to you that really hurt you and triggered negative feelings about yourself. Years may have passed, but whenever that incident rears its ugly head in your memory, your heart plummets into your gut.

Write about that time when you didn't love yourself.

Did the words that hurt you come from someone you knew well?

____

____

How did it affect the way you view yourself?

____

____

How did it affect your relationship?

____

____

What did you learn from that experience?

____

____

How has that experience shaped you into the person you are today?

____

____

Have you forgiven the person who said hurtful words to you? If not, why not, and how can you get there?

Did the person who said those awful things to you say them with good intentions, or did the person say them out of spite?

It's important to make that distinction. Understanding where that individual is coming from can help you start healing that wound. While it's important to go through the emotions while we struggle – the anger and the tears – sharing an emotionally charged message before you've worked through the mess may not be beneficial to your audience, or yourself in the long-run. When you share a story from a scar, instead of a wound, you've done the work to learn from the difficult experience and have the clarity to share knowledge that can help others.

LEARN TO LOVE YOUR VOICE

> "The only way to find your voice is to use it."
> – Jen Mueller

"You won't make it in television news unless you work on your voice."

My eyes grew wide as my mouth snapped shut facing the news director who was reviewing my portfolio of on-camera work as a student. His feedback ripped my pride to shreds. "Huh?" My brow furrowed as I thought to myself, "My voice? I thought my voice was one of my best assets!"

After a short pause, I spoke, ready for more feedback: "Alright. What else can I work on?"

"You have to do everything you can so that when you walk into a room, you own it. That means try acting and modelling."

"Excuse me?" My inner voice interrupted, as I stared at him blankly. "ME? Act and model? I was called the ugliest girl in school in Grade 8. Making that happen is as possible as a snowball's chance in hell!"

The news director's advice was a hard pill to swallow. He was paired up with me as a mentor at a national Radio Television Digital News Association (RTDNA) conference for broadcast journalists. I was getting ready to graduate from the broadcast news program at SAIT. While I could have brushed off his opinion, I knew he wasn't far off-base. My voice was naturally high pitched and thin. All the broadcaster voices, both male and female, that I heard on TV were low and rich. This advice was coming from a person who held the keys to an industry I desperately wanted to enter.

After hearing the news director's opinion, I could have trapped myself thinking "My voice isn't low enough, I won't be able to be a broadcast journalist." Instead, I took his advice and took action because I wanted to break into the TV news industry so badly. After the conference was over, I signed up with a talent agency and got to work on myself and my confidence in front of the camera.

My voice was a hurdle in front of my goal, and I did whatever it took to clear it. No one was going to come and save me. I had the power to improve it with hard work. Whenever there was a print story in front of me, I would hold it up and practice reading it out loud every single day. Newspaper articles, magazine ads, children's stories – I used everything I could get my hands on to improve the way I presented and the sound of my voice. I practiced vocal exercises and learned breathing techniques to strengthen my voice. I auditioned for acting gigs. And something wonderful and unexpected happened! I was cast as a co-host of a non-profit organization's promotional video. With every step outside of my comfort zone, my voice and my confidence were getting bigger and stronger. Giving up was not an option, especially when I was so close to my goal. When you know the direction you want to head towards:

Find a way forward. Even if it means *failing forward*. It's better than quitting and *falling backwards*.

Have you ever listened to a recording of yourself and immediately thought "Is that actually what I sound like?" Sorry, the recording isn't lying. I used to feel the same way about my voice. I sounded like a child.

What matured my voice was hard work, age, and experience. And if you don't already love it, you can learn to love the sound of your voice with patience and practice.

My friend Brendan McDermott teaches film and broadcasting as well as broadcast journalism to high school students. Brendan's the kind of teacher you'd want to have, and you'd remember him years after taking his class – that's what his former students have told him. A passionate storyteller, he's experienced and excellent at what he does.

At the start of every school year, Brendan shows a video to his film and broadcasting classes that I voiced when we were in school together at SAIT in 2007. My voiceover is part of a 60-second public service announcement for the Rainbow Society of Alberta, a non-profit organization that helps grant wishes of children diagnosed with a severe chronic condition or life-threatening medical illness in the province. The project has been near and dear to Brendan because it gave him a chance to give back to the Rainbow Society. His cousin was born with a heart defect, and they granted her wish to go to Disney World. Brendan uses this video as an example to teach his class about story-structure, script-writing, and the creative process. He also uses it as an illustration to teach his class about the power of being vulnerable when sharing a personal story.

As part of the lesson, Brendan shows his class my picture, explaining my journey from student to news anchor and morning show co-host to owner of a video production company.

Brendan believes you never know where you're going to end up:

> "We grow, change, and adapt. In a million years, I never thought I would be teaching, especially broadcasting. Kids feel like they need to map everything when in fact they need to chill and experience life. I went from TV, back to school, to Corporate Communications and brand management, back to school, and now I live in a classroom. I feel that I have the best of both worlds – storytelling and sharing that passion with my kiddos who are going to be our next generation of storytellers."

Brendan says the feedback he gets about my voice can be all over the map, "Students are always honest and willing to share their insights, even when us adults don't want to hear them." Brendan's right. Kids are truth-tellers. Honesty keeps us humble. While some students consider the way I voiced the project as professional, the comment from a student that stopped me in my tracks was, "She sounds like Siri."

"Oh my gosh. Do I really sound like that?"

I had to find out for myself. Brendan graciously allowed me to include this story in the book and sent me the video after I interviewed him. I watched it 14 years after I voiced it, and paid close attention to my voice. I wish I could say the student was wrong, and that I actually sound like the female version of James Earl Jones. Come on, who doesn't love the legendary actor's deep, buttery voice? His voice has brought iconic characters including Darth Vader and Mufasa to life. The uncomfortable truth is my voice in that video project really sounds something like the original voice of Siri. Go ahead and laugh – I am!

When you over-articulate each word, sounding conversational goes out the window! I sounded like the voice from a software program.

Before I beat myself up too badly, I want to remind both of us that we're all a work in progress. The way I sounded in my early twenties as a student is not what it is now in my late thirties after I worked hard to improve it.

Understanding the science behind why you don't hear yourself the way others do helps put things in perspective. When you hear your voice on a recording, you're only hearing sounds transmitted through air conduction. When you speak and hear your own voice inside your head, you're also receiving the sound a second way – through the bones and tissue in your head that tend to enhance lower-frequency vibrations. This means that your voice usually sounds fuller and deeper to you than it actually is.

The good news is you can get over the feeling of disdain for your own voice, which is important if you plan to show up confidently in video. Take the time to record yourself speaking and then listen back to it. The more often you do it, the more you'll get used to it and train your brain to love your voice. When I started training to be a broadcaster, I recorded myself speaking and listened back to it. I eventually got the courage to ask mentors for feedback. After watching and hearing myself many times, I got used to the way I looked and sounded and actually felt excited to see myself on screen. When you practice and exercise patience, the same thing will happen to you too.

Your voice is powerful. It can be used to uplift people, give a voice to the voiceless, and connect with others. In a world where you can be anything, be kind – including to yourself.

Love your voice, because there's a chance that if you don't then no one else will.

Your voice is a gift. It's not too late to learn to love it.

My voice isn't perfect – but it's mine, and I've learned to love it. Let me tell you about a cool full-circle moment.

As an Apple device user, I've asked Siri lots of pressing questions. Imagine how pumped I felt when Susan Bennett, the very real woman behind the original voice of Siri, followed me on Twitter! I fangirled pretty hard when that happened!

Brendan and I in 2021

REFLECTION EXERCISE ON RECOGNIZING BLOCKS

How do you feel when you watch the playback of one of your videos that you're in? What do you think of your voice? If you have any doubts, or negative feelings about seeing yourself and hearing yourself in videos, try the following exercise to shift your mindset. Start by writing down your obstacle in first person, using "I". Then rewrite that same statement in third person to distance yourself from that negative feeling. Lastly, flip the script and turn it into a positive statement referring to yourself as "I" or "me". The following is an example of how I've reframed my internal narrative about public speaking using this exercise:

Example statement in first person:
I had an embarrassing public speaking experience and now I know I can't do it again.

Example statement in third person:
Felicia had an embarrassing public speaking experience when she was 17, and now she wants to hide whenever she's asked to perform in front of an audience.

Example of flipping the script:
I had an embarrassing public speaking experience when I was 17, but I'm learning from my mistakes to become a great public speaker who is also compelling on camera.

Now it's your turn to do the exercise.
Example statement in first person:

____

____

Example statement in third person:

____

____

Example of flipping the script:

____

____

The way you describe yourself is powerful. When you describe yourself accurately in a positive light, you can acknowledge and appreciate your own wonderful qualities. We can be our own worst critic. Perhaps the following statements sound familiar:

"I'm not qualified enough."
"I'm not pretty enough."
"I'm not skinny enough."

And then there's the other end of the spectrum.
"I'm too qualified."
"I'm too old."
"I'm too young."

We often carry around negative beliefs that we're either too much or too little of what we think we need to be to make our goals a reality. There's also a chance that someone stuck their limiting beliefs on you. If you want something badly enough, you'll need to banish those beliefs and have the courage to try.

For instance, some of my biggest blocks to get into TV news were:

"I look too young."

"I'm not experienced enough."

While there wasn't much that I could do about my baby face, I knew that eventually my chubby cheeks would disappear. To beef up my resume, I would have to gain experience by seeking out opportunities that not everyone wanted. Tenacity, hard work, and professionalism helped me to overcome what I saw as early deficiencies. Later in my journalism career, I was often sent out to do stories on young people. The cool thing was the young people I interviewed had an easier time relating to me because of the way I looked. What was once a setback had become an advantage.

Over to you. Fill in the blanks with what has been stopping you from creating videos.

"I'm not ______________________________ enough."
and/or:
"I'm too ______________________________."

Imagining false scenarios hurt your feelings and your potential. With practice, the weight of those false beliefs will become less of a burden as you gain confidence on screen and behind the camera.

What you see as a shortcoming could actually be a strength that helps connect you with your unique audience

When you change the story that you tell yourself *about yourself,* you have the power to change your life, and captivate an audience with your story.

PREPARING YOUR VOICE AND BODY TO PERFORM

Warmups aren't exclusive to athletes preparing for a big game; they're important before you perform in front of a live audience, and before you hop on camera to record a video. Warming up your voice and your body before delivering your message will help to align your body, decrease nerves, boost your energy, and magnify your presence on screen.

Vocal warmups stretch your vocal cords, loosens muscles used to articulate words, and helps clear your throat. I'm going to keep vocal exercises simple by teaching you what I use to improve my voice. Try the following warmups to see if they work for you:

Humming – Humming is an easy and gentle way to warm up your vocal cords. Relax everything, including your lips, jaw, neck and shoulders. Sit or stand up straight and with your lips gently closed, take a deep breath and exhale while humming a "hmmm" sound until you're out of breath. Repeat this exercise five times.

Jaw and mouth loosening exercises – Many of us hold a lot of tension in our jaws. This warmup will stretch your facial muscles in different directions, improving articulation while loosening your jaw so it's easier to speak. While sitting or standing straight, find the two joints where your jaw opens and closes at the base of each ear with your index, middle and ring fingers on both of your hands. These are your temporomandibular joints. You may be able to find these spots easier when you open and shut your jaw. Massage both sides of your jaw joints by making small circles with your fingers while you say:

- **MRO** – pronounced "mmm-row" – exaggerate your facial movements while you repeat MRO slowly ten times.
- **BN** – pronounced "B-N" – exaggerate your facial movements while you slowly repeat the letter B followed by N ten times.

Once you've warmed up your voice, focus on loosening up your body and getting pumped up to perform. It's important to move your body before you do a presentation live or pre-recorded because it helps increase circulation and boosts the oxygen going to your lungs and brain, which makes you perform better.

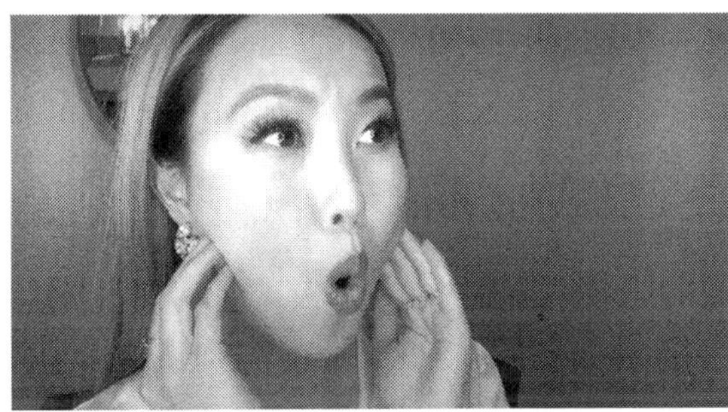

Demonstrating the MRO exercise

Boost your energy

Every day before going on TV, I would warm up my body in the makeup room or in the washroom when no one else was around. Knowing that I could make strange sounds and do high kicks in private helped me loosen up before a show. Possessing more energy in your delivery is important when you're delivering a message. The camera drains your energy, and it can make you look less interesting to watch. To combat this, bring your energy up a few levels from your normal way of speaking.

These are fun ways to get moving while boosting your energy:

- Put on your favourite tunes and dance.
- Imagine you're a boxer, or a martial artist, and throw some powerful punches and kicks.
- Jump up and down to release nervous energy.

When you're recording, using your hands helps you look more dynamic. Use hand gestures with intention. When you use a prop, make sure it has a purpose and illustrates a point.

Remember to smile

Smiling is powerful. Of course, if you're making a sad or serious video, nix the smile. However, if you're delivering a positive message, smiling while you speak creates an audible change in your voice. Not only does smiling impact your voice, but the person also hearing and seeing you smile will automatically smile back.

Stand up straight

As a teenager with low self-esteem, who spent a lot of time studying at a desk, I often hunched over. "Stand up straight, Felicia!" my aunt would remind me each time she saw me. She was onto something. Not only do you look more confident when you have good posture, you sound more confident too. When your back isn't lined up it's harder to get enough breath to support your voice when you need to project it.

A relaxed back in a vertical position, with knees slightly bent and head held up high gives you the proper posture to look confident on camera and improve your vocal quality.

The power of pausing

Imagine watching speakers who don't take a breath as they jump from one idea to the next. It can be hard to watch.

When people don't pause, it's easy to tell that they're nervous and it gives the impression that they want to get the presentation over with. Pausing is powerful. Pauses act as periods when you're expressing ideas verbally. Pausing gives a cue to your audience that what you just said is important and provides more impact to your message. When you pause, remember to breathe. Breathing fills your lungs up with air so there's more support for your voice, making it easier for those listening to hear what you're saying.

One of the most common concerns my students have is being self-conscious about saying "um" and "ah" during a presentation. If you recognize that you use these filler words a lot, slow down and pause. Slowing down allows your mind and your audience to catch up to what you're saying. And when you get nervous speaking, remember to slow down and pause after each idea and breathe.

Be conversational

No one likes listening to someone who sounds like a robot. When I was in university, my organic chemistry professor put many of us to sleep with his dry delivery of the course material. I couldn't stand it any longer, so I switched classes to listen to a different professor. When you don't want to put people to sleep while you're speaking, be conversational.

It's the easiest way to kick a monotone delivery to the curb. If you're recording a video of yourself speaking, think of the camera as your best friend that you're having a great chat with. When you want to boost your connection with an audience remember:

The lens is your friend.

To look more engaged in your video, look directly at the camera lens and not at yourself on screen. Doing this will make you look like you're speaking directly to the person watching your video.

Drink plenty of water

The best thing to drink when you're getting ready to present is water. Staying hydrated helps your body lubricate your vocal cords, which vibrate when you speak. While the water you drink doesn't directly contact your vocal cords, the temperature of the water makes a difference on your voice. Put the ice-cold water back in the fridge when you're about to speak for a long time. Cold water can tighten your vocal cords and decrease your vocal quality. Warm to hot water – but not so hot that it hurts you – helps to keep the muscles around your vocal cords limber.

VIDEO EXERCISE TO GET USED TO YOURSELF ON CAMERA

Using the performance tips in this chapter and the shooting and editing tips from the previous chapter, let's continue building your confidence on camera.

Record a video of yourself speaking on camera every day for the next week. It doesn't have to be long.

You can make a video out of each of the reflection exercises from earlier in this chapter. Each video can be about you sharing a short story from your life.

The goal is to get used to the way you look and sound in video. Every time you finish recording a video, play it back. Try to record the videos in a single take. With more practice, you'll get used to speaking more clearly and concisely and that will make it easier to edit your videos.

What do you love about yourself in your videos?

____

____

What is one small thing you can improve for the next videos you record?

____

____

I'm proud of you for taking steps to help grow your on-screen confidence. After you record a video, post it to Instagram or TikTok and tag me @reelawesomeproductions so I can cheer you on! I'm in your corner!

FIND YOUR CHEERLEADERS

Surrounding yourself with people who believe in you and will stand by you makes a huge difference when you're stepping outside your comfort zone. When I was getting ready to graduate from the broadcast news program and was starting to look for work, I attended a RTDNA Prairie Region news conference with a plan. Even though this was a smaller version of the national conference I told you about earlier, I would have to be bold and network because meeting a news director at this conference could help me land my first job as a broadcaster. It wouldn't be a walk in the park. I would be competing with lots of new grads who also wanted to break into the industry. Thankfully, I had help from someone who believed in me. My instructor at the time, Shelly Blore, walked straight up to Carl Worth, who was the news director of CTV Regina, looked him in the eye and said, "Carl, this is Felicia Yap. You're going to want to hire her." Now that's what I'm talking about! Having people on your side that will root for you makes such a huge difference. After that awesome introduction, and a nice conversation between us, Carl was open to looking at my work.

I mailed him a DVD of my work and, soon after he watched it, Carl called to tell me about an opportunity to work as a video journalist in Yorkton, Saskatchewan. Carl explained it was a starting place for young journalists to gain lots of experience with limited resources. I only had experience living in a large city, so I'd have to get used to living in a small city in comparison to what I was used to if I got the job. First, I'd need to pass a phone interview with the station's news director at the time, Bob Maloney.

While speaking with Bob I got a good sense of his warm and caring personality, and my gut told me that his station would be a good place to kickstart my career. Then Bob said something that made my dreams a reality.

"You got the job!"

My jaw swung open. "This is the best news! Thank you. THANK YOU!"

It was a glorious fist-pumping moment. There were too many times before where I felt like the underdog – unworthy and unwanted. The odds of breaking into the industry were against me, but I bet on myself and won! This was a triumph! It happened because I didn't give up, and I was encouraged by an amazing group of people who believed in me. Both Bob and Carl have played a big part in shaping me as a storyteller during my early days as a journalist.

I reconnected with both Bob and Carl while writing this book. Bob said the staggering number of applications he got for jobs at CTV Yorkton was a challenge, and that only the best candidates made it to the actual interview process. When I asked Carl why he gave me a shot after we first met, he said, "I just liked you. There was an upbeat joy to you, then and now – a joy in how you are and in how you see the world. And when I watched your work for the first time on that DVD, I knew you could do it."

Wow. I was truly moved when I heard that. Carl has always had a way with words and has always been one of my greatest supporters. I'm forever grateful to Carl, Bob and Shelly who believed in me and allowed me to prove to myself and the naysayers that I could achieve my dreams.

Carl and I in the CTV Regina newsroom in 2010

Before you start posting videos of yourself to boost your business, tell the people who you trust the most about your plan along with the fears and doubts you may have about sharing your message. Not everyone you confide in will understand what it's like to create videos to amplify an online presence. That's okay. The people that you want in your corner will help lift you up during difficult times, and they'll cheer you on during the highs and lows. My friend Emily Chase is someone who I'm glad to have in my corner. When I started my YouTube channel, she'd often share my videos on Facebook. Having her love and support has made a big difference riding the wave as a digital content creator. I'm excited to share Emily's story later in this book.

Feeling worried or scared about sharing videos of yourself to spread ideas you're passionate about is expected. It's only human to feel this way.

I'd be lying if I said I didn't think about whether people would like my videos and would follow me on social media. When you want to break out of this slump, remind yourself there are roughly eight billion human hearts beating now. The odds are in your favour that you and your message will connect with many people!

There will be days when you would rather clean toilets, cook a five-course meal from scratch, or write an essay – basically do anything else but create a social media post. You're not the only one who feels this way. A great motivator is this: do it for the people you serve with your message. When you include more than yourself in the equation, it becomes more pressing to share your stories because of your mission. There are people who may not like, comment, or repost your content, but they're quietly watching and deciding in private if they want to take the next step to work with you. There are also people who will publicly cheer you on. Show up for all these different members of your audience because it shows them that you care. You never know how you and your work can impact a life. When someone does tell you, it feels extra good. For example, I recorded a video about my personal reasons for writing this book that include being a role model for my daughters and one that my younger self would have looked up to. The video really resonated with my Instagram follower, Karen Jennifer Li who is a social media consultant and the CEO of her own company AskMe Social.

Karen connected with my message and responded with this comment about why she shows up on social media:

> "Ahhhh! This video is making me tear up. I echo your truth. My "why" is always for my younger self too. It hurts to rarely see people who look like me in the social media industry and I want to continue to show up for the younger me, the future generations, and my peers. I appreciate you so, so much, Felicia."

I wanted to tear up when I read Karen's message. Her words moved me to believe that being myself is enough to inspire others, and that sharing my own message can make a difference in someone's life. At the time that she posted that comment, the only interactions I had with Karen were written messages and comments over Instagram. We live in different countries. Yet by showing up authentically, I was able to make an impact on her. Since then, she's become more than one of my followers. She's a friend. We've connected through video, built a positive relationship, and continue to cheer each other on. That's part of the power of sharing your story through video on social media: you can connect with someone and make a difference. And when you lift your connections up, they will often do the same for you.

INTROVERTS CAN BE CONFIDENT ON CAMERA

You can develop an unshakeable confidence in your own voice and grow your online presence – even if you're introverted. Hear me out. In kindergarten, I was so quiet and shy that I didn't have a single friend in class.

Even though I was born an introvert, I've been able to do extroverted things by breaking out of my shell time and time again. You can be successful on video without changing your personality.

Creating videos when you're genuine and true to yourself is much more sustainable. Also, people want to connect with you – the real you.

Make being true to yourself a guiding principle. It has been for Jamie Kern Lima, the founder of IT Cosmetics. She started the beauty line in her living room, and grew the company into the largest luxury makeup brand in the US. In her book, *Believe It,* she writes: "Realizing the power of authenticity takes so much pressure and stress off. Because there is only one you. And being anyone other than yourself simply won't work. Realizing this sets you free."

If you don't fit into a mold, stop trying.
Never look for where you can fit in.
Instead, look for where you can stand out
because you've been made to shine.

POSITIVE MINDSET

When you create videos, choose to believe in a positive outcome. Visualizing success boosts confidence. When you imagine every step of the process working out, you prepare your mind and body to take those steps in real life. There have been so many times in my career as a news anchor where I felt overwhelmed delivering the details of breaking news coming in at the last second or covering major stories and was tempted to think "This is going to be awful!"

However, whenever I visualized a newscast turning out awesome, instead of focusing on what could go wrong, it usually did turn out to be an awesome show!

Whenever creating a video makes you think "I dread this," flip the script and say "I get to do this" instead. Beginning with a positive mindset will set you up on the right path.

EMBRACING YOUR AGE ON CAMERA

> "I look forward to being older, when what you look like becomes less and less an issue and what you are is the point."
> – Susan Sarandon

Several women who are 40 and above have shared with me that their insecurities about the way they look holds them back from showing up on screen. They don't feel as confident in their appearance as they did in their 20s or 30s. If you're worried about your age and wrinkles showing on camera, remind yourself of the invaluable wisdom and experience you bring to the table! You have lived so much more life than someone in their 20s or 30s has.

Take a moment to think about the individuals you admire. Are they still finding their footing, or have they walked many steps and found their way in life? The people who I look up to have become experts in their field through many years of experience, and often their age shows. I'm not following them for what they look like. What about you? Do you admire a mature person for their heart and wisdom, or for their appearance?

The world is ready to see more mature-looking people on social media. I've seen so many grandmas and grandpas who are being themselves on camera and the world loves them for it. I hope this helps to convince you that:

Being older doesn't make you obsolete; it opens opportunities to share your wealth of knowledge and heart.

Choose to be brave. We can't get back time wasted trying to be perfect and being trapped by the fear of judgement. If you need encouragement, take a lesson from my 67-year-old mom: "When I was younger, I was too scared to speak up or speak with people I didn't know. I was worried about being judged. As I got older, I stopped caring. Now I can talk to anyone. I don't care what they think of me."

My mom lives her life this way. To know her is to love her. Standing five feet tall, don't let my mom's stature or her soft, raspy voice fool you. She's a tiny woman with a big personality and an even bigger heart. She makes friends everywhere she goes, including the owners of local Chinese restaurants. We often get special dishes and treatment at these places thanks to my mom!

The days of scripting my videos word-for-word are long gone. I've learned trusting in myself and sharing the real me allows me to create more videos in less time and helps me to connect with my audience in a more authentic way. Stop letting self-doubt cage you in.

When you decide to believe in yourself, you give yourself permission to open the latch and feel the freedom to spread your wings and fly!

Begin where you are.
If you wait until you have everything figured out to start, you could be waiting for the rest of your life.

After reading the last chapter, you have the fundamentals of how to shoot and edit mobile video. And by doing the exercises in this chapter, you'll become more confident in the way you look and sound on camera. In the next chapter, you'll learn how to structure your own unique story to captivate your audience and why sharing your own stories is powerful.

KERRI CUST ON PUTTING YOURSELF ON THE MENU

If you want to start radically loving and appreciating the person staring back at you in the mirror and on screen, pay close attention to self-love coach Kerri Cust. She wants you to do more than simply accept yourself – she wants you to celebrate who you are. Wanting to boost her own confidence on camera and to learn skills to create her own videos, Kerri was one of my very first Video Confidence Academy students. As we got to know each other, I learned that Kerri is passionate about teaching women to truly love and trust themselves. I'm delighted to include her story and her insight on self-love in this book.

While there's been a wave of people adopting a mindset to detach themselves from the way their body looks at any given time – known as "body neutrality" – Kerri says doing this creates a flat energy about yourself. She encourages you to ask "What do I really love about myself and my body? What can I really celebrate? When you do this, you shift from that flatness to an energy that's more active." As an example, Kerri really loves her dark hair. She recommends focusing on at least one thing you love about yourself, internally or externally, that's worth celebrating. As for me, I genuinely love my smile because it can cheer people up. I also love my voice because I can use it to encourage others and share stories with it. Kerri says focusing on something you really love about yourself changes how you show up on camera and how you feel about it.

You'll be more willing to shoot a video when you love something about yourself, and that makes it more appealing to the people who watch your video. It also gives others permission to do the same.

Kerri says learning to love yourself is a journey and not a destination. Her journey to loving herself truly began in 2013 after her life was flipped upside-down – going through a divorce and losing her brother all within three weeks. She packed up and moved from Canada to the other side of the world and joined a yoga community on the island of Koh Pha Ngan in Thailand for a few years, where she was forced to face her body insecurities. Kerri says a large birthmark that covers her whole left arm made her want to cover up her body all the time. Growing up, she chose to wear long sleeves vacationing at the lake, and in gym class even when she was feeling hot. But in Koh Pha Ngan, the sweltering conditions made wearing long sleeves unbearable. So, the layers came off, and instead of getting the negative reactions she expected, the community didn't make a big deal of what she tried to hide her whole life: "The weight of it went away. I've been carrying this for 30 something years. Instead of pushing it away and hiding it, it's like 'Hey I'm really insecure about this, and I step forward with it anyway'."

Kerri's top three tips to love yourself more so you can show up confidently on camera are the following:

1. **Put yourself on the menu** – In other words, choose yourself. Make fulfilling your needs and desires a priority so you can be the best version of yourself.
2. **Turn up the volume on the positive instead of the negative** – Negative rhetoric will always exist, so instead focus on the aspects of yourself of which you're proud (both internally and externally).

3. **Surround yourself with a solid supportive community** – Engaging with people who encourage and love you will increase your level of confidence and self-love.

When you don't feel like recording a video, try the following tips from Kerri that'll put you in the right space to hit record:

1. **Remind yourself of the truth** – Remember the wonderful things people have said to you that you know are true. Give yourself a pep talk.
2. **Dance and have fun** – Play music that you love and move your body to it. Shooting videos doesn't have to feel heavy. Dancing shifts your energy and the way you feel about yourself.

Kerri says when we show up from a more fulfilled place, we can be more inspiring to others. Letting go of the doubt and shame is liberating. While nurturing self-love takes time and practice, it's worth the journey and makes it much easier to show up on camera to share your message.

You can learn more about Kerri at kerricust.com.

Chapter 3
HOW TO SET YOURSELF APART FROM EVERYONE ELSE

"The only way to do great work is to love what you do. If you haven't found it yet, keep looking. Don't settle."

– Steve Jobs

I tell stories for a living. I've interviewed thousands of story-makers, including Olympic medallists, Academy Award winners, high-profile politicians, scientists, and savants. You're a story-maker too. You might not fall into one of these high-profile categories, but I know in my heart of hearts that you are damn interesting, with a wicked story to tell! In this chapter, you'll learn how to craft your unique story in a compelling way, why your personal stories set you apart from everyone else, and how to document them effectively so you can make good use of them in different scenarios.

Even if you don't believe that your story will change the world, *I guarantee your story will change someone's world.*

THE POWER OF STORIES

> "Out of suffering have emerged the strongest souls; the most massive characters are seared with scars."
> – Kahlil Gibran

It's not the stories involving big names that have made the biggest impact on my own life. Quite the contrary. One of the most unforgettable stories I've covered as a journalist was about a young entrepreneur at the end of his life. He was blessed with the looks and charm of a movie star, without the notoriety. He and his wife, and two young children made a picture-perfect family. And, for a while, at least from an outsider looking in, all was perfect. He left a promising career in banking with a big paycheque to be his own boss. He taught himself to build homes from reading books. He told me one of his proudest moments was when he sold the home he built with his own two hands. While he was focused on growing his business, however, life threw him a curveball.

It was melanoma.

He beat it once, but it came back angry and with a vengeance. Wincing, his body shook as he carefully stretched out on a couch for our television interview. I opened my eyes wide in hopes of holding back tears from falling down my cheeks as I listened to his journey and thought about what cancer stole from him. He was so brave.

It takes incredible courage to be vulnerable and share your heart during dark times. He confessed that in his younger days, he spent a lot of time outdoors without enough sun protection. Doctors removed a growth, the size of a tennis ball from his back.

The prognosis: two months to live.

His purpose had now become crystal clear. His goal was to make as many memories as he could with his family before his last breath. He was going to try everything he could to improve his health and extend his life to be with the people that mattered most. His community came together to start an online fundraiser for his family to help lighten the financial burden while he and his wife weren't working. He said before cancer showed up, he'd ask his children to wait whenever they wanted to play so he could finish up work, but this life-changing diagnosis made him realize how precious and limited both life and time are.

He decided to shift his priorities so that he would drop everything to play with his kids. To be honest, I don't remember his name and I don't know the details of what happened after his story aired. But that's not the point. What stuck with me is the experience of being with him as he shared his story and the lessons his story taught me. There have been many times when my kids want my attention while I'm working. That temptation to stay focused on a project is strong, but his story reminds me of what's important: life can change in an instant, work will always be there, and children will only be little for a little while. His story also showed me the importance of doing what you love. These are powerful teachings that I would have never learned unless he had shared his story. Stories have the power to connect us and inspire us to be better human beings.

American entrepreneur and *New York Times* bestselling author, Marie Forleo, hit the nail on the head with these words: "It's hard to be what you don't see." So, hold a mirror up to that glorious face and precious life of yours! It's time to count all the blessings you have and the remarkable things you've done and will do. There's greatness in you. You may not see it yet, but that's because:

We are usually the last to realize how truly awesome we are.

Realizing our own greatness often starts by pinpointing when and how we learned important lessons. It means recognizing the life-changing experiences and ordinary moments that pushed us to the place we wanted to be. Even as a professional storyteller, it's much easier to tell someone else's story than my own. Telling my own story through this book has been a mammoth-sized undertaking, and the most difficult project I've taken on to date both professionally and personally. It's the first time I've taken the time to document my experiences and put them under a microscope in order to share what I've learned.

By now you have an idea of how I went from being a student to getting my first journalism job. But the part of my story that's coming up next will explain why I left a professional career that I loved to become an entrepreneur. I hope sharing it will help you realize that it's okay to pivot and choose to grow with new challenges.

TURN "EXCEPT" INTO "ACCEPT"

"Finding your passion isn't just about careers and money. It's about finding your authentic self. The one you've buried beneath other people's needs."

– Kristin Hannah

What was your first job like? Mine consisted of driving for hours alone on unfamiliar back country roads to small towns and places unmarked, equipped with camera gear and a keen sense of adventure. It included interviewing strangers, making lifelong friends, and incredible once-in-a lifetime experiences such as flying in a helicopter, a private plane, and travelling in an antique Bombardier Snow Bus that broke down a few times in knee-deep snow during the dead of winter. While I got lost a lot (I have a terrible sense of direction), in many ways I found myself in Yorkton, Saskatchewan.

I bulked up on valuable experience on the anchor desk and went into the field to cover crime, sports, farm stories, and politics. The work was tough, physically and mentally and could be emotional at times, but I loved it. My starting wage as a videographer was roughly $13 an hour. I drove a base model Toyota Corolla without air conditioning and automatic windows, because I don't like spending outside my means. My extended family still gives me a hard time about that car, but in my defence, it was dependable, and took me to some amazing places across North America. My monthly budget for groceries was $120. I dined on homemade sandwiches and iceberg lettuce salad almost every day. I worked long hours and weekends.

Most on-air personalities working in Canadian TV news will likely tell you it's not a glamorous life. Choosing this career isn't about the money. The work filled my soul and, in that way, I was rich.

But my personal life was in the dumps. Everyone I loved – my family, my friends, and my new boyfriend (who was Andrew) were all a ten-hour drive away in Calgary. My coworkers were very kind and lovely people, but I still felt lonely. *So lonely.* When work was done, I would call home and I would often end up crying because I missed home and, frankly, I missed people. It was the first time in my life that I had lived on my own. I was used to always having someone to turn to and hang out with.

Being too proud and stubborn and "thrifty," I refused to buy a proper mattress and had a sore back from sleeping on an air mattress for months on end.

"Why should I buy a good mattress?" I reasoned, "I'll only be here for a few months before I get my next job and then I'll have to get rid of it."

I was sorely mistaken. Four months passed, and there were no takers. I applied to bigger stations. No one in charge would give me a chance. They called me too green and too young.

Starting my career in a small news market allowed me to have so many incredible experiences because I was one of only two journalists working at the TV station. I didn't have to compete with others with more experience or talent than me. We had to rely on each other to get the work done. I gained so many amazing memories that I wouldn't have had if I hadn't started where I did. In the front of my mind, my clear career goal was to return home to Calgary to tell stories.

It wasn't until I was sitting in church during a short visit home that I heard this message – "Transform your *except* into an *accept*."

When I returned to Yorkton, I put that message into practice. Instead of thinking "I love my work *except* I live far from everyone I love," I turned that "except" into "I *accept* that I live far from home for now and it's part of my journey." After that mindset shift, amazing things started happening! Greg Ottenbreit, Member of the Legislative Assembly for Yorkton, invited me to his church after one of our interviews. Longing to be part of a community, I agreed.

The congregation welcomed me with open arms, and I ended up becoming good friends with a few members of the church. The loneliness I felt when I first moved to Yorkton disappeared because of the life-long friendships I made at work and in the community. As an example of the kind of people I worked with, one of my co-workers gave me a king-sized mattress once she learned I was sleeping on an air mattress. My back was saved! I learned an important lesson – that when you move to an unfamiliar place, build a network. Give that place and the people in it a chance.

With experience and hard work, my confidence on camera and in making videos grew; and those in charge of hiring noticed. Carl Worth offered me a job to work at his station in Regina, a middle-sized news market. I'd be filling in a one-year maternity-leave position as the late-night anchor.

It took an extra eight months longer than I thought it would, but I was finally ready for my next big step. Over my last few days in Yorkton, I cried. Except now I wasn't sad about my life there – I was sad about the supportive community and friendships I was leaving behind.

Working at a larger station came with new benefits and challenges. I was closer to home, and there were more opportunities to gain experience on the anchor desk and producing longer newscasts. There was a larger team, and I became friends with many of my teammates. I learned how to deliver the weather off a green screen, which was tricky when I first started. The audience was larger, and that meant more people were willing to voice what they really thought of my on-air performance. I had to learn that the public's feedback, good or bad, came with the job.

Once my one-year stint in Regina was over, I took a big leap of faith by accepting a seven-week gig across the country in a larger news market. I packed two suitcases, took my first-ever flight to the East Coast, and touched down at the Halifax Stanfield International Airport in Nova Scotia. My partner, Andrew, was living in Fredericton, New Brunswick, at the time, which made our long-distance relationship seem less far apart. CTV Atlantic delivers regional newscasts for the Maritime Provinces – Nova Scotia, New Brunswick, and Prince Edward Island. The news director of CTV Atlantic asked me to stay after my temporary job was over. So I flew back to Regina with Andrew, cleared out my apartment and we drove my Corolla on a fun road trip through the United States back to Halifax. I eventually earned a full-time position at the station and worked my way up from being a weekend weather specialist and late-night anchor to a co-host and anchor of the morning show and noon-show anchor.

As I became more established as a journalist, I didn't have to look for jobs; news directors came to me with opportunities. An American talent scout who watched me on the morning show tempted me with an opportunity to move my career to the States. While it could have been an exciting adventure, I turned the talent scout and the idea down.

I didn't want to add anymore distance and strain on my relationship with Andrew. Andrew and I had a plan to make our long-distance relationship work. By the time he finished medical school, we would have done six years of long-distance. Enough was enough. We decided that wherever he matched to his residency program to continue his medical training, I would leave my job and move with him.

We wanted to start a family and decided that living in the same city as my supportive family would be the best scenario for us. At the tail end of medical school in Canada, students apply for a specialty program. There's a chance medical students won't match to their chosen program or, worse, won't match to a program at all. When match day came, Andrew and I sat in front of his laptop, and took a deep breath in unison as he clicked on the result. Andrew sped through the words so fast, I couldn't keep up.

All I heard was the most important word, "Calgary."

"CALGARY?" I held my breath in disbelief.

"We matched to Calgary!"

We jumped out of our seats and hugged. I cried. "I'm going home!"

After seven years of working in different cities and missing my family endlessly, I was over the moon to be moving home and to finally be living under the same roof as Andrew!

FINDING MY PURPOSE AGAIN

2015 was a big year of changes. Andrew was wrapping up medical school. He and I were getting married in Mexico and moving across the country to Calgary all within a few weeks of each other. While I was excited to get my personal life in order, I was sad to leave CTV Atlantic. It had been my home for five years. I planned ahead for the transition, and had a part-time reporting job lined up in Calgary. But I found out just four days before I was supposed to start that a round of layoffs meant my plan fell through. It had been my dream to tell stories in the city I grew up in. I worked so hard for seven years in different cities to get to this point in my career, and the opportunity that would make that dream come true vanished. This sucker punch knocked me off my feet, but I didn't stay down for long. Something life-changing was about to happen.

"Check it again."

"It's positive."

"Are you sure?"

"Yes!"

"We're going to be parents?" Andrew nodded with a big smile as he held up the pregnancy test. I burst into tears. My heart was full. Just in case you haven't noticed, I'm a sensitive soul. While one of my goals in life was to be a journalist, the other one was to be a mom. I recognize that I'm very blessed to have been able to conceive a child, and I don't take that for granted. After I found out I was going to be a mom, I shifted my focus from my career to caring for my family. I knew my workaholism, combined with taxing shiftwork expected in TV news, meant that going back to that career wouldn't be the right choice for me and my growing family.

Months later, after a long and difficult labour and delivery, Aurora was born as the sun was rising. Her name means "dawn" or "first light." When the nurses placed Aurora on my chest for the first time, an overwhelming rush of wonder came over me. Blame it on the surge of oxytocin because it was love at first sight. Eyes wide open, she looked up at me and smiled. I melted. I could no longer be selfish and think only of myself. She needed me just as much as I needed her.

Becoming a new mom turned my world upside down. While I read books and did parenting courses, experience was my best teacher. While most of my focus was on being a mom and raising Aurora, I spent some of my time and energy building my DIY YouTube channel *Most Delightful Way*. I'm crafty and artistic. I even made the tulle skirt I'm wearing on the front cover of this book. On my YouTube channel I shared budget-friendly ways to create gorgeous wedding décor, easy recipes, and fun baby costumes. Offers to collaborate with international companies trickled into my inbox. People were watching!

I continued creating DIY tutorials for another two years until I didn't have enough time or energy to keep it going. Free time was even harder to come by after our second little girl, Gwyneth, joined our family two years later. Her name means "happiness" and "blessed." She embodies both of these qualities. My girls are my enthusiastic sidekicks. I love how I can do life with them!

I thought I knew what being sleep-deprived was while I worked on a morning show. But it pales in comparison to the repeated wakeups every night from a newborn and a toddler. I had two sleep disruptors – one on my hip and the other on my lap. Being a mom has been the most difficult and most rewarding role I've signed up for.

Between the diaper changes, cleaning never-ending spills, playing, and teaching, I made little time for myself – and thereby made myself little. While life as a stay-at-home mom brought me so much joy, over time I realized something was missing. That something was me. Although I personally know women who are working moms, and others who are stay-at-home moms, and they are all incredible mothers who are also incredible individuals, and I appreciate and admire all of them, my passion and sense of self-worth were getting lost in the busyness of motherhood.

As soon as I left my career in broadcast news, I started having a terrible recurring dream for an entire year. I would show up at my desk in the newsroom but discover someone else sitting in my seat. I had been replaced! I didn't belong anywhere. It was more than a bad dream – this was a nightmare. This dream eventually faded, but another recurring dream took its place. I'd find myself studying with a group of people, and then realize I was preparing an application to medical school. This dream came in slight variations, but the feeling was always the same. I was scared and stressed about applying for medical school. "What the heck?" I wondered where these thoughts were coming from. "Medical school? Talk about a blast from the past!"

I spent many nights wide awake, unable to sleep because I couldn't stop thinking about what to do with my life. I felt like I wasn't fulfilling my purpose and I wasn't meeting expectations of myself. It had been four years since I stepped away from my career. I felt washed up, but I wasn't ready to throw in the towel.

I loved being a mom, but I wanted to do something else as well – just for me. I was ready to act. I didn't know what to do until I decided to simply *do something*.

Stop taking the supporting role.
You were made to be the hero of your life's story.

I knew I loved creating and hosting videos. That's why I started *Most Delightful Way*. But, the craft projects I created for my channel were piling up around the house and collecting dust. I was spending more money buying materials for projects than I was making on YouTube. Some of my videos would take days to finish. I didn't want to spend that kind of time on something that wasn't bringing me joy or the results I wanted anymore. I was wrestling so hard with what to do with my life *again*, so one day I decided to sit in stillness for a while and thought about what really makes me happy. A quiet and clear voice spoke to my heart: "Storytelling sparks joy in your life. Do that." After listening to that advice, a sense of peace fell over me and I thought to myself "That's so right! I miss telling stories. I'm good at video storytelling. I love inspiring, entertaining, and improving lives through the stories I tell. Storytelling makes my heart sing!"

By the end of 2019, both of my daughters had become a little more independent and I was getting a solid stretch of five hours of sleep now. Woo hoo! Five hours of uninterrupted sleep! Studies have shown adults need at least seven hours of quality sleep on a regular basis. Getting less than that has been linked with poor health, including weight gain, heart disease, and depression.

But for the first time in years, I was sleeping better and that was a game-changer because getting good sleep is magical!

I kept revisiting the idea of launching a videography business because I missed video storytelling so much. Even so, the fear of failure pulled me back. "No one knows or cares who I am, where I am now," I thought, sitting silently with my head in my hands on my living room couch. "I went from being nearly a household name in the Maritimes to being a nobody in my hometown."

Video storytelling was in my wheelhouse, but running a startup company was not. My parents owned a business and they had to file for bankruptcy. My older brother co-owned a business selling produce at a farmers' market, but it wasn't financially viable so he ended up closing shop. "Being a successful entrepreneur isn't in my blood!" my inner voice told me. "I don't think I'll be good at it. I don't know anything about business. What if my idea is a flop?" The worst thing I could have done is to listen to my negative thoughts. I would have been stuck in my head and would have nothing to show for it. But when that happens:

Get out of your head and get moving.

So, I did. I got off that couch and I did something. For months, I spent many hours creating videos at no-charge or for very little to help friends with businesses and non-profit organizations. I thought "Money will come, but the experience and testimonials to bulk up my portfolio are priceless." I used the video and audio equipment that I already owned to keep costs down. Producing videos is time consuming, but so much fun!

One of the hardest parts of starting my own business was coming up with a name. Have you ever tried securing a website domain, only to find almost everything you'd thought of is taken or being held hostage by domain pirates? It's incredibly frustrating! After two months of relentless brainstorming, it hit me like a lightning bolt. "Reel Awesome. REEL AWESOME!" I immediately checked the domain and found out it was still up for grabs. Oh, the relief!

It was a perfect pairing of videography and the feeling I want people to have when they think of my brand. I launched Reel Awesome Productions during the COVID-19 pandemic in 2020. It was an uncertain time for the whole world, but I was tired of "What ifs." I flipped the switch and started living with "WHY NOT!" My long-standing dream has been to tell stories in the city I grew up in. I may not be doing it in the way I originally planned as a reporter and anchor, and it's taken me longer than expected, but I'm thrilled to be making my dream happen my way!

Following a dream by only doing what you love, though, can only get you so far. You need the skillset to pull it off. This intersection between your talent and passion and values is the sweet spot. If you have the drive but not the skills yet, do whatever it takes to learn those skills to make it happen. Invest time and money in yourself because:

You are your most important investment.

Are you're thinking "What if I don't have the time? What if I don't have the money?" If it really matters, you'll find the time and you'll get resourceful if you don't have the money.

There are endless opportunities to learn about virtually every subject online, and often at no cost. Find a way to make your goals happen, no matter what.

Videography, on-camera communication, interviews, and storytelling are my forte. Business is not. I took online courses and workshops galore to beef up my business knowledge. That's how I met marketing coach Lyndsie Barrie, the founder of YYC Fempreneurs. I enrolled in her marketing school.

She encouraged me to share my story and my business. I've met so many amazing female business owners and professionals through her community, and I wouldn't have been able to until I decided to step out of my comfort zone and invest in myself. Starting a new journey can be lonely, so one of the best things you can do is:

Surround yourself with like-minded people and you will belong.

The more promo videos I produced for entrepreneurs, the more I noticed something they had in common. They told me such things as:

"I'm really awkward in videos."

"Please help me look less awkward."

"Being on camera is so hard."

What I heard is that they didn't feel confident on camera. Speaking on screen stressed them out. Thankfully, with my interviewing and hosting experience, I knew how to calmly guide them to on-camera confidence. "Aha!" A light bulb switched on in my head. "I'm really good at this, and people need this!" It was something exciting and different.

I saw a need that was being unmet in an area that I excelled in. I also learned that some of my clients wanted to learn how to shoot and edit videos themselves, which was right up my alley. I pivoted my business to include coaching people how to show up authentically and confidently on video to grow their online presence. I'm empowering big-hearted business owners and professionals with the tools they need to make their dreams come true – and it feels so good!

If you want to learn valuable video skills in a structured way, check out my Video Confidence Academy course, or if you want personalized coaching go to my website **reelawesome.com** for more information.

Ever since I decided to get out of my head and lead with my heart, I've felt whole again. The missing piece of the puzzle was filled by pursuing my passion. The terrible nightmares of finding myself kicked out of my spot at work have completely stopped. Thank goodness! I no longer feel lost. If you ever feel this way, stop making excuses and start being braver because:

When you share your magic with the world, you'll go from feeling irrelevant to being irreplaceable!

My journey to becoming a video confidence coach has involved big leaps, in geography and in courage. If you're still contemplating what is your next step, you may be surprised that the answer has been within you all along. One of my oldest and dearest friends, Jennifer Vuong, dug out our Grade 6 yearbook and she showed me my entry, about a quarter of a century after it was made. I had forgotten all about it.

We had been asked to describe our favourite things, our family, our school, and what we wanted to be when we grew up. I took one look at what I wrote under the headline AMBITION and was floored! This is what I had written:

> "I would like to be a journalist, because I like to write reports on the topic I am doing. This is my life."

Mind blown! If only I could have consulted 11-year-old me! She instinctively knew what she wanted to pursue, and for some time I had abandoned her when I couldn't hear her anymore over the opinions of others. I think about all the years spent torn over what I should do with my life. Sometimes the answer we've been looking for has been within us all along.

Sometimes realizing our dreams for the first time, or the second time later in life is for the best. Life's a rollercoaster ride. If it were a train ride chugging down a straight track, it would be boring. It takes longer to arrive at the destination, but it is the twists and turns that shape us into who we need to become to be ready to take the next big step. Those detours make life interesting and oh so exciting!

If you often find it hard to decide what to do because you're passionate about several things, know this: while it would have saved time knowing that I should have stuck to storytelling instead of trying to become a doctor, if I was given a redo I wouldn't do anything differently.

I hope you take the time to write out all the twists and turns and unexpected sudden stops in your life like I have in this book. And I hope that what you see makes you want to do it all again in a heartbeat.

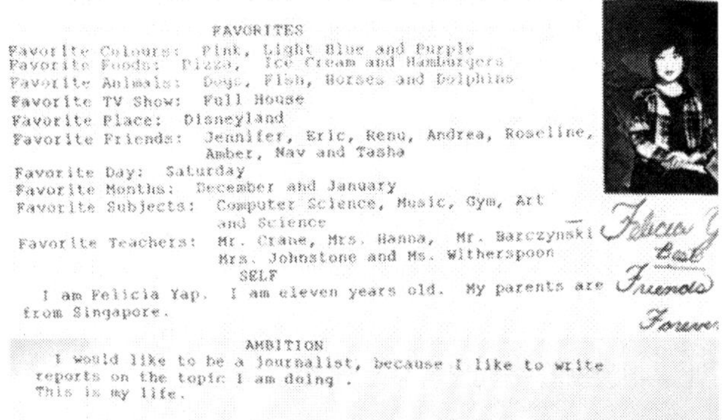

FAVORITES

Favorite Colours: Pink, Light Blue and Purple
Favorite Foods: Pizza, Ice Cream and Hamburgers
Favorite Animals: Dogs, Fish, Horses and Dolphins
Favorite TV Show: Full House
Favorite Place: Disneyland
Favorite Friends: Jennifer, Eric, Renu, Andrea, Roseline, Amber, Nav and Tasha
Favorite Day: Saturday
Favorite Months: December and January
Favorite Subjects: Computer Science, Music, Gym, Art and Science
Favorite Teachers: Mr. Crane, Mrs. Hanna, Mr. Barczynski Mrs. Johnstone and Ms. Witherspoon

SELF

I am Felicia Yap. I am eleven years old. My parents are from Singapore.

AMBITION

I would like to be a journalist, because I like to write reports on the topic I am doing. This is my life.

Part of my Grade 6 yearbook entry

DEVELOPING YOUR FINGERPRINT STORY

Harnessing the power of your story boosts the impact of the content you share to market yourself and what you offer. People buy products and services from people they trust. If you haven't already, it's imperative that you nail down your own story – the short version of the one you're going to tell prospects over and over again because it gives context.

If I hadn't shared the story in the introduction about feeling confused about what I was supposed to do with my life and how I almost didn't follow my heart to get to where I am today, would you want to learn from me?

Would you trust me to guide you if you didn't know some of the hardest challenges I overcame?

Do you know anyone else who has a story exactly like mine, about an Asian girl who was told not to follow her dreams by a loving aunt, feeling like she'd let her parents down by not getting accepted to medical school and then went on to become a professional storyteller and television presenter?

I have a strong hunch you answered "No" to all of the above. That's because each of us has a story that's one-of-a-kind. Let's get to work on crafting yours so you can share it with the world.

Your fingerprint is unique to you – so is your story. Your experiences can't be replicated. They've led you to where you are, what you do, and who you are now. Your fingerprint story is your origin story and your elevator pitch rolled into one, and it should showcase your character and competence.

REFLECTION EXERCISE ON DEVELOPING YOUR FINGERPRINT STORY

Write down your answers the following questions to craft your own Fingerprint Story:

How did you learn your special gift that makes you stand out? Were you fed up? Fired? Inspired? Did you suffer an injury or loss? This is the driving force behind your story.

What is the moment or experience that led you to that point? What caused you to make the leap to pursue your goal? Describe how you felt in detail.

Why are you in your current role?

How does your knowledge, talent, product or service improve lives?

Arrange you answers together to create your Fingerprint Story. Here's some space to write it down. If you need more room to brainstorm, or to write out a draft, use a separate sheet of paper or save it as a digital file.

Look at what you've written. How do you feel about it? Does it make you excited enough to share it? If it does – AWESOME! You have just created the script for an important piece of video content that introduces new audience members and potential clients to you!

After reading this chapter, you know the big and little details of my story. You'll notice that my Fingerprint Story is a condensed version, and I leave out the details that don't add value to it. Your Fingerprint Story should only cover the important points too. With that in mind, here's an example of how answering the framework questions helped me to develop my own Fingerprint Story:

How did you learn your special gift that makes you stand out?

I spent 20 years gaining industry on-screen experience and behind the lens as a videographer and was inspired to use my skills to help business owners and professionals become confident on video and in making videos.

What is the moment or experiences that led you to that point?

I saw many of my connections and clients who offer amazing products and services, scared to be featured in their videos and overwhelmed to create videos themselves.

Why are you in your current role?

I made the leap from TV news anchor, morning show co-host, and reporter to entrepreneur after becoming a mom, and this allowed me to do what I love while raising a young family.

How does your knowledge, talent, product or service improve lives?

I empower big-hearted business owners and professionals with the tools and support to show up and share their unique message and gifts with the world.

Organize your answers in an order that flows. In my case, I start off with what I do for clients and how I improve lives. Then I explain the experiences that led me to the point of becoming a videographer and video confidence coach.

Next, I talk about how I learned my special gift that sets me apart from my competitors. Finally, I describe what made me take the leap to be in this role. I'll show you what I mean.

Felicia's Fingerprint Story:

> I'm Felicia Yap, a videographer and video confidence coach who empowers big-hearted business owners and professionals with the tools and support to show up and share their unique message and gifts with the world. As my business grew, I saw many of my connections and clients, who offer amazing products and services, scared to be featured in their own videos and overwhelmed when they tried to create videos themselves. I realize that I have the unique ability to guide them to video confidence with my 20 years of industry experience on screen and behind the lens. I made the leap from television anchor, morning show co-host, and reporter with CTV News to entrepreneur after becoming a mom, allowing me to do what I love while living a life I love!

Your story isn't set in stone. You can decide what to share. The experiences that you include don't have to be life-shattering or dramatic; they just need to come from a genuine place and be connected to why you do what you do. As you change, so does your Fingerprint Story.

Refer to your Fingerprint Story when you need help focusing your message. If you found this exercise hard, what's hard about it? Are you clear about your story? Do you know who you help with your product or service? The exercises in this book will be more useful to you once you have a clear vision of what you do, why you do it, and who you serve.

VIDEO EXERCISE ON YOUR FINGERPRINT STORY

Shoot a video of yourself sharing your Fingerprint Story. Please tag me @reelawesomeproductions when you post it to Instagram or TikTok so that I can support you by sharing it with my viewers.

TOSS THE STARFISH

> "Great stories happen to those who can tell them."
> – Ira Glass

Presentations can fall flat when they only target their audience's brain. Sticking to straight facts misses the mark. Have you ever watched a presentation, live or recorded, that jumped from facts to figures and back to facts again?

Yawn.

Maybe you remembered one of the stats, but unless you have a photographic memory you'd be hard pressed to regurgitate the presentation to your best friend who hasn't watched it yet. Why? Because the speaker forgot to aim for both your head *and* your heart. There were no emotional moments, no jokes, no photos or videos of people, and no story arc to carry the audience through the beginning, middle, and end of the presentation.

Startling statistics can be shocking, but often they can be too abstract and it's hard to feel them. Including facts becomes so much more memorable when they're wrapped in a story. People care about facts when they understand how they impact others. For instance, inflation means more than prices going up, it means low-income and vulnerable people are going to be struggling even more.

When you have a personal connection and are passionate about the topic, you'll be more engaging because you're engaged in the material. Make the story yours, down to the last detail.

If you find the topic or story that you're spreading truly interesting and wonderful, there's a greater chance your audience will too because:

Inspired people inspire people.

I'm going to share one of the most embarrassing moments of my life to illustrate how it taught me one of the most important lessons that I teach to my own students who want to be confident communicators.

Imagine you're 17-years-old and you've been asked to deliver a speech in front of thousands of people. You do the work to prepare and rehearse, but it all goes horribly wrong when it counts. This sums up what happened to me. If you want the details – read on my friend.

My high school graduating class was big. Two valedictorians were hand-picked to give speeches at our graduation, and I was one of them. I bounced in my seat as I got to work on crafting the perfect speech.

While I had some experience emceeing school concerts and making announcements over a school intercom growing up, I didn't have any formal public speaking training, so I searched HOW TO WRITE A GOOD SPEECH online. A website suggested adding a story to make the speech interesting. The theme of our graduating class was "The future belongs to those who dream," so I wanted to include a story that would inspire my classmates.

I read several short inspirational stories online and picked the "Starfish Story" originally written by anthropologist and nature writer Loren Eiseley. The story has been adapted and retold by many motivational speakers.

Here's one version:

> One day a man was walking along the beach when he noticed a boy picking something up and gently throwing it into the ocean.
>
> Approaching the boy, he asked, "What are you doing?"
>
> "Throwing starfish back into the ocean. The surf is up and the tide is going out. If I don't throw them back, they'll die."
>
> "Son," the man said, "don't you realize there are miles and miles of beach and hundreds of starfish? You can't make a difference!"
>
> After listening politely, the boy bent down, picked up another starfish, and threw it back into the surf.
>
> Then, smiling at the man, he said "I made a difference for that one."

This story about the power of making a difference was a perfect fit! I believed practice makes perfect, so I practiced and practiced my graduation speech until I could recite it with my eyes closed.

The big day arrived.

"Break a leg, Felicia!" One of the bigwigs gave me the thumbs up as all of the VIPs of the graduation ceremony lined up to parade on stage. I was one of them.

"Thanks, I can use all the luck I can get!" I said, beaming. This was a huge deal.

The center of the auditorium floor was transformed into a royal blue sea of caps and gowns. Crisp air circulated through the massive space, mixing with the buzz of indistinguishable chatter from excited grads.

Guests flanked the wings of the main floor and filled the seats all the way up the dimly lit balcony levels.

Bright lights made it hard to make out faces from a distance, but I could read homemade poster board signs with oversized words, CONGRATULATIONS, YOU DID IT!

With one of the best seats in the house, I stared wide-eyed into the packed auditorium from the stage, as nervousness and excitement rose within me. Scanning the room, it took a few minutes to spot my family. It was nearly a full house. They found seats on the top level of the auditorium, waiting for my turn to take the podium and to walk across the stage. The pressure to perform turned my stomach into knots, but I knew I was well prepared. "You got this, Felicia!" I told myself. "Take in everything so you can remember this amazing day and this monumental moment."

Shoulders back, head lifted, I basked in the glory of being chosen to speak. That is until the keynote speaker delivered a line that didn't literally or figuratively break my leg, but it did break my pride.

"One day a man was walking along the beach when he noticed a boy picking something up and gently throwing it into the ocean."

Gasp. "WAIT. WHAT? What is happening?" My mind went numb. The speaker continued:

"What are you doing?"

The boy replied, "Throwing starfish back into the ocean."

"OH NOOOO!! No. No. NO! I can't believe this is happening! He stole my story! I don't have another story! What am I going to do?" His words, amplified by the microphone, were drowned by waves of panic crashing through my body. All the hours spent rehearsing didn't prepare me for this unfortunate twist. My gown grew heavy as my confidence dwindled.

The bright lights hanging above, carving out thousands of silhouettes, grew painfully blinding.

Eyes shut, drowning in anxiety, I pleaded with the stage to swallow me whole. Then the speaker's words cut me again.

"I made a difference for that one."

Colour drained from my face. "He's getting close to finishing his speech. What can I do?," I worried. "My whole speech is written around that "Starfish Story." I don't know how to change everything at this moment. I'll have to stick with the plan, but my plan sucks! ARGH!"

Thunderous applause interrupted my run-on thoughts. The keynote speaker returned to his seat. He had hit a homerun, and I was envisioning stepping up to the plate with an automatic three strikes before I even swung.

The room grew quiet again, but inside I was screaming "I don't want to do this!" But I had no choice, this has to happen. The emcee walked up to the microphone and delivered a brief introduction about me.

"Here is Felicia Yap."

That was my cue. Hands shaking and feet dragging, I peeled myself off my seat and gathered every ounce of my courage at the podium.

The hours of practicing helped me stay composed as I spoke into the microphone, but as I got closer and closer to the "Starfish Story" I wanted to turn back.

With flushed cheeks, I looked down while these words left my lips: "One day a man was walking along the beach when he noticed a boy picking something up and gently throwing it into the ocean." I let a nervous chuckle escape with the words. It was my way of letting everyone know what was coming.

I felt the weight of thousands of eyes on me as I finished repeating the same story they had just heard a few minutes earlier.

Every word that I repeated was like a red-hot poker sticking into my side, and my cheeks flushed in the same hue. It took all my strength and willpower to finish the script.

"Congratulations, Class of 2001."

Polite applause capped off my speech. I stepped away from the microphone feeling a lot smaller than then when I first walked on the stage.

I didn't have to wonder for long about what people really thought of my speech. They told me.

"How's the starfish doing, Felicia?"

"Don't forget about the starfish!"

UGH. Both my speech and I were a joke. My peers were laughing at me. It sucked so much. What should have been one of my proudest moments turned into a complete flop. It would be seven years before I would be given the opportunity to redeem myself.

In 2008, I was chosen as the valedictorian to give the graduation address for my faculty, the School of Information and Communications Technologies at SAIT. Call it poetic justice or a crazy coincidence, but I would be delivering my speech on the same stage at the same venue as when I was graduating high school. This time I was determined not to make the same mistake from my high school graduation speech.

Armed with an extra seven years of life experience since my last graduation speech, I packed my speech with personal stories that no one else would be able to replicate.

Thousands of people filled the auditorium for the graduation ceremony. "Here we go again!" I thought. Was I nervous? Yes. Was I confident? Definitely!

Being prepared and knowing that my message was unique made all the difference. That message was live your life with no reserve, no retreat, and no regret.

I didn't want to embarrass myself again by using a popular story I found online, so each section of the message included personal experiences and stories.

While it had a personal touch, I also made the speech about my audience and how they could be inspired to live a purpose-filled and powerful life. And you know what? Something awesome happened! At the end of my speech, the entire audience rose to their feet with a roaring round of applause! It's a pinch-me moment that's etched into my memory. After the other speakers, dignitaries, and I walked off the stage, no one teased me. Instead, they showered me with compliments about my speech. Thank goodness!

I'll never look at starfish the same way again. Don't get me wrong – I love starfish. They're beautiful and remarkable creatures. Starfish can regenerate limbs and, in some cases, entire bodies. I doodle them every time I imagine an underwater world or decorate a beach scene for my girls. But after the "Starfish Story" was linked to my most embarrassing public speaking moment, they have claimed a special status in my life. They serve as a reminder of both what not to do and what to do when making a public presentation.

The "Starfish Story" was never mine. Because I was unable to see the power that my own stories and experiences would have had on my audience, I chose to borrow someone else's story when I was 17. The truth is we lose our power and authenticity when we rely on someone else's work. The power of your own personal story trumps sharing someone else's story every time.

So the next time you're honoured with an opportunity to speak, remember to toss the starfish and:

Let the power of your personal story shine.

You don't have to constantly look outward for content inspiration. Most of your best material is within you. Don't focus on telling your entire life story. That's much too daunting. Tell a small personal story, one at a time. It's much easier to start this way. You have a collection of stories stored in your mind that are ripe for the picking.

It's time to pluck a few of your best life stories out of your head and put them where you can easily see them all in one place. Keeping your stories together will make it easy to reference them when you need them.

A STORY RECIPE: HOW TO SHARE EXPERIENCES FOR MAXIMUM IMPACT

Think about memorable moments in your life. I'm sure you got a lot of them! You may be wondering how to tell your own stories to make an impact. By using my Story Recipe, you can cook up a collection of your own experiences that can help others – and yourself. You may brush-off your experiences, thinking they're not worth sharing, but I want to show you how to structure your stories for maximum impact so that you can recognize them as valuable.

The collection of your experiences will help you in several situations. When you're asked to give a presentation, you can review your collection to see which of your experiences will help to illustrate a point. You can use the ideas to create compelling videos. And you can even review your Story Recipe collection to help you prepare for an interview. Using my Story Recipe framework can help make you more relatable.

If you're being interviewed for a job or on a show, knowing your pivotal stories ahead of time will help prove what you're capable of when you're asked for examples by the interviewer.

Every time you experience something unforgettable, add it to your collection. Keep records of your experiences together in a place that you'll remember, so you can easily reference them when you need to do so.

Not only can you turn these experiences into videos, but you can also re-purpose them as audio or written content. Super useful, right? Well, here are the list of ingredients and directions for the Story Recipe to help you structure your stories with maximum impact:

Ingredients:

Short name
Elements
Key points
Value

Directions:

Short name – Whip up a catchy, short title that'll jog your memory whenever you see it.

Elements – Sprinkle in the details to establish the experience by answering these questions:

Who?
What?
When?
Where?
Why?
How?

Key points – To make it relatable, fold in the negatives about the experience and the positives. To make the story valuable for your audience, explain what you learned as the frosting on top. Bonus points if you can add a splash of humour.

Negatives
Positives
Lesson(s)

Value – Finish with how sharing this experience would help someone.

If you follow this recipe, you'll have the basis for a solid story that you can proudly serve to prospects.

Here's an example of how I structured the story about my valedictorian speeches using my Story Recipe:

Short name –

- Starfish Story

Elements –

Who?

- A 17-year-old me, and then a 24-year-old me

What?

- Keynote speaker used the same story as I did for my valedictorian speech when I was 17
- Valedictorian speech at SAIT included personal stories

When?

- High school convocation and convocation seven years later

Where?

- Both at the Jubilee Auditorium in Calgary

Why?

- Conflict happened when I used the "Starfish Story"

How?

- Asked to give a valedictorian speech for my high school that ended up as a flop
- Was able to redeem myself on the same stage seven years later

Key points –

Negatives:

- Embarrassed after the keynote speaker delivered the same "Starfish Story"
- Peers mocked me after my high school speech

Positives:

- Got to speak in front of big audiences as a valedictorian twice in my life
- Didn't give up public speaking after a negative experience
- Received a standing ovation after my speech at SAIT

Lesson:

- Personal stories are powerful and set you apart from everyone else

Value –

- To help people realize the power of their own stories
- To inspire people not to give up after an embarrassing public speaking experience

Following the Story Recipe allows you to pull all the important and impactful details from an experience and lays it in front of you so you can recognize its value. Next, take all the information you entered and turn it into an engaging story that you can use for video content.

Now for some heartfelt advice about deciding what content to create. Focusing only on your audience and forgetting yourself and your interests in the process can be exhausting and less enjoyable for you. At one stage, I put in all my energy into publishing new DIY tutorials every week on my YouTube channel. I wanted to grow my channel and collaborate with cool companies. My subscriber count climbed to more than 11,000. My craft videos often took 10 to 20 hours to create, including the conceptual stage, scripting, shooting, editing, and then finally publishing. While I was able to keep up the pace with one baby, I lost steam when I had my second daughter and decided to pull back on the volume of videos I was creating because of burnout. My *why* wasn't strong enough to keep going. At that point I realized creating craft tutorials didn't spark the same kind of joy that it once did. If you're juggling a family, running a business, and maintaining a social media presence – I get you. It's super hard to keep all the balls in motion, especially when you're running on empty. So whether you're just starting out, or have been producing videos for years, keep the following in mind:

Sustainable video storytelling is a happy medium between giving your viewers what they want and giving your creative soul what it needs to thrive.

Your life and the stories in it are a gift, so share them. You don't have to be famous to have your life stories change lives. Your life story is your legacy and should be passed down.

By keeping your stories and message a secret, you are actually denying someone who could really benefit from hearing your story. Now that you're building a collection of experiences, let's take them and make them into videos that work for you.

Chapter 4
YOUR STORIES IN YOUR STYLE

"You're never going to kill storytelling, because it's built in the human plan. We come with it."

– Margaret Atwood

"Attention over here! Attention over here!" a five-year-old me cried, waving at my dad in hopes he would shift from recording my little brother to me. It's a snippet from a simple video documenting my family at home many moons ago, but I still get a kick out of it every time I watch it. While I was too shy to speak to strangers as a little girl, I hammed it up for the camera. My love affair with making videos and being in them started when I picked up my dad's black Sony camcorder as a child to record everyday moments and school projects. Being able to watch and re-watch unique and everyday pieces of the past on a screen is such a gift, and something I still don't take for granted.

How much of your time, energy and money is spent online?

If you're like many of us, significant transactions and connections are made on the internet, and time can be gobbled up quickly using it.

With a multitude of eyeballs sifting and scrolling through an ever-growing body of information and distractions, harnessing the power of video to magnify your message can help set you apart from the crowd because the medium quickly grabs and keeps attention. There are many different styles of video used on social platforms. Figuring out which styles work best for you will boost your confidence and give you more options to create and get you visible. Video creation is meant to be fun! By the end of this chapter, you'll have plenty of practice creating with multiple videos in the bank.

VIDEO STYLES

The videos you create are limited only by your skill and imagination. The more you practice making videos, the more comfortable you'll get and that will allow you to push your own boundaries to tell powerful stories. If you've been stuck idling, here are some ideas to get you moving from merely thinking of producing videos to actually making them. These videos fit into two categories:

1. On-camera
2. Off-camera

On-camera videos

One-spot talk – This style of video for a solo speaker works well for delivering information directly to the audience. To do this style, stand or sit in one place, stabilize the camera, and look directly into the camera lens when you speak.

One-spot talk video

Walk and talk – When you want to incorporate movement into a video, you can record yourself talking while walking and holding your phone with your hand or camera stabilizer such as a selfie stick. The movement and changing background can make your video more visually interesting.

Walk and talk video

Demonstration – This style of video shows the viewer how to do something, such as tutorials, dances, and cooking demos. The person or people in the video aren't staying in one spot, they're moving.

Place your camera far away enough from the action and the speaker to capture this style of video.

Demonstration video

Co-hosting – When there's another person who can discuss and engage in a topic with you, the two of you can co-host a video together. Shoot wide, from a further distance, to include both people on screen.

Co-hosting video

Interview – The interview style of video usually involves two speakers: a host and a guest. It can be formal or casual, while educating and/or entertaining an audience through the discussion of a topic.

When you pre-record interviews, you can either shoot them in person, with both people next to each other in the same room, or remotely, with both speakers in different places using a program that allows video conferencing.

Interview video on Instagram Live

Off-camera videos

Hands only – This style of video is a demonstration type video which focuses on hands without a person's face. A voiceover helps to move the video along.

Pictures and sound – A compilation of moving still images or footage is combined with sound, such as music or a voiceover, to create this style of video.

START WITH YOUR AUDIENCE

The confidence tips in this book are meant for on-camera videos, where you show your face on screen. But if producing off-camera videos helps you ease into shooting and editing videos or provides more variety in the types of videos you make, then go for it! You can go a lot further once you find a shoe that fits. Once you've landed on a style that you love and are working towards mastering it, then switch to another when you want to add variety.

Videos come in different forms, but high-performing ones share a common trait: the audience is the foundation. That means building content that helps the person watching solve a problem, learn something new, or feel something deeply. Coming up with content that benefits your audience doesn't have to be complicated. Make your life easier by starting with what they want. Doing research to see what's engaging people in your industry will take much of the guesswork and frustration out of your content creation. One of the simplest and most effective ways to do this is to ask your audience for feedback. Ask them what they want to know more about, then think about how you as an expert can help them with that topic. One powerful question you can ask is:

What is the greatest challenge or frustration that you are dealing with when it comes to ___________?

For example, in one of my videos I asked my Instagram followers what their biggest challenge was when it comes to video creation.

Members of my audience spoke up with these fantastic responses:

"Uploading in high def. Instagram is horrible for that."

"I feel limited by my technology. Tell me it's possible to shoot and edit good video content on an iPhone?"

"Not knowing what to say or how to articulate what I'm trying to say!"

Turns out technology struggles affected a lot of the people who responded to my question. Another issue that some people voiced is the issue of presenting with confidence. But the most common challenge among those who shared their biggest challenge with video creation was coming up with fresh ideas for content:

"For me, I struggle finding new and creative content every day. I'm not sure who told me that I should be posting every day, but it really has been difficult trying to achieve this."

"Oooh, good question. Content is a big one. Coming up with something new when there are so many new and emerging trends ALL the time. It can be hard to keep up. How do you stay ahead without burning yourself out?"

"Content. Content. Content. Did I say content?!?"

Bingo! With these responses I created four distinct videos addressing the issues facing my audience. Because I posed a question, they told me exactly what they wanted, and I was able to provide it and ultimately help them and others who are facing the same challenges. The feedback to these videos was all positive. Other viewers chimed in because they found great value in the content. The best part – it's easy! People love it when you ask them for their input because it makes them feel involved and, in general, people love to help when they're asked for it.

The beauty of this strategy is your audience will likely bring up challenges that you may not have anticipated. To give you an edge over the competition:

Stop guessing.
Directly ask your audience what they want help with.

SHARE WHAT YOU KNOW

Everything you experience has potential to be shared. Major life-changing events are obvious material, but don't gloss over ordinary moments that can be just as meaningful and entertaining. It's in the small stuff – the little everyday moments – that life is truly lived. What you may consider humdrum could become a viral video when done right. Think about the types of videos you've shared. Was there an adorable baby in one of them? Did one of them include a pet doing something funny? Maybe you saved a budget fashion tutorial. None of these videos are earth-shattering, but they still have the power to pull us in, and make us laugh or cry – so we spread them like wildfire. Why? One powerful concept – relatability.

A lifestyle influencer, for example, could share her favourite healthy brunch recipe that's passed around on a golden platter during family gatherings. Did you catch why this story stands out? I wove the brunch recipe in with a story about why it's meaningful. Family gatherings are special events where memories are made. The brunch recipe could help the viewer make special memories with their own family. Pointing out the value in the video tells the viewer why they should pay attention instead of scrolling past it.

A mompreneur could switch things up from posting about her new product by sharing a video tutorial about how she gets her makeup done in less than five minutes, in between getting breakfast ready for the kids and rushing out the door for morning drop offs. Many women would be hooked with the promise of looking fresh-faced in under five minutes. Giving the audience a glimpse of the morning chaos behind her as she buffs in her foundation and layers on a sheer coat of coral on her lips, before her toddler snatches her lip balm and takes off with it, makes it that much more relatable and entertaining. And remember, you get to choose how you want to be portrayed in your own content. If you and your family have decided that your kids are part of your brand, then include them. Set your boundaries and build your content around them. If you're wondering about how much of your life you should share, I explain more about building healthy boundaries at the end of Chapter 8 with my friend Emily Chase.

People love experiencing new things, even if they can't physically be there with you. So why not take your audience with you when you try something new? If there's value in it for them – it's a story worth telling. Going live as you step into a brand-new bakery in your neighbourhood to fawn over the dainty blush décor and the macarons worthy of a wedding magazine cover can be great content. As a sign of respect, ask for permission before recording video on someone else's property. You could answer questions and respond to comments from those watching as they trickle in, as you take your audience along for the ride – from the service at the till to the first bite of that raspberry macaron you've been dying to try. Mmmm. Yum.

When you don't have a plan and you're not sure what to talk about, broadcasting live can be scary. However, having some talking points beforehand will give you more confidence than winging it. Publishing videos after you record them is fine too. Recording footage while you're experiencing something, and then posting it later, still takes your viewers behind the scenes, making them feel special. If you want more tips on how to broadcast live with confidence, read Chapter 5: How to Light Up a Room.

When you struggle to come up with content ideas, keeping an eye on what's trending is one approach. Taking note of videos by your favourite influencers with lots of views and engagement can help. Outward inspiration often jumpstarts ideas; but if you want to create meaningful content with ease, then look inward. The content that comes most naturally to you is what you already know. When we speak without being boastful and from a place of experience, we share our humanity. Of course, stories with universal themes that others can connect with have wider appeal. So, if it feels like you're hitting a brick wall to come up with content ideas, step back and:

Share what you know.

Sometimes your mess is your message. Not all the stories that you choose to share will be sunshine and rainbows. Some of the most powerful stories are often the most difficult to tell. Emotional stories can create unity and inspire action. Sharing difficult experiences sends a message of hope: "If I can do it, so can you!"

Most people would prefer not to talk about an assault from a trusted relative, a car crash that ended the life of a loved one, a medical emergency, or something else that haunts them. If you're a trauma survivor and reading this – know you're incredibly strong and resilient. If, how, and when you decide to share traumatic memories is very personal. Self-disclosure is important therapy for some, and others would rather keep their past private. Either way is fine. That being said, the world is hurting. People are hungry for connection. Sharing real and raw stories is needed now more than ever.

CLARIFYING YOUR CONTENT

Everything is content. All the things that happen to us and around us, good or bad, can be a story worth sharing. When you're deciding on the idea for a piece of content, run it through this litmus test by asking: "What is the value of this content for my audience?"

Content is valuable if it adds something positive to someone's life. For it to do that, it should accomplish at least one of the following:

- Educate
- Entertain
- Engage
- Inspire
- Promote

I'll go through each of these in detail.

Educate

Teach something you know! What's a topic that potential customers need help with that you can explain? What information can you share that can improve someone's life? What's something new in your area of expertise that your potential customer doesn't know about yet?

For instance, I help people learn to love their own voice so I researched the scientific reason why our voice sounds different in recordings compared to what we think we sound like. I created a short educational video about that topic, and that video received lots of engagement and thousands of views.

You don't need to do research for a video if you already know the subject well. I've published several makeup tutorials related to looking camera-ready because teaching how to look good on camera is something I have experience in, and I know how to do it well.

Entertain

The world needs more joy and laughter. Deliver entertainment value by creating videos that'll get viewers to burst out laughing or at least will turn frowns upside down. Entertaining videos are highly shareable and will help to boost your reach to a larger audience. By showing your potential customers that you understand where they're coming from, and what they're going through, you'll be able to build trust and relationships with them.

I was inspired to create an entertaining video when I started writing about imposter syndrome – the feeling of not being good enough and doubting your abilities despite past accomplishments. The ink flew out of my pen while I wrote a rough script, before squeezing into my two-piece canary skirt suit that I used to anchor the news in. And then I sat my tush down in front of my ring light and hit the record button on my phone.

News anchor: "Glad to have you with us. We begin with breaking news. Authorities have captured the culprit believed to be responsible for robbing the confidence many of us should have in ourselves. Let's watch this exclusive interview with the accused."

Imposter syndrome: "Your talent and experience don't matter. They're going to figure out you're a fraud. You're not good enough."

News anchor: "Experts say there are ways to lock imposter syndrome up for good. They include not fearing failure, taking action to gain confidence, and to stop thinking like an imposter."

"Gosh, this is fun!" I felt like my feet barely touched the ground while recording the video. I was in my happy place. I delivered the message in my news anchor voice, which is louder and deeper compared to how I usually speak.

I had such a great time making that video and resurrecting a skill that I used to use all the time. Viewers connected with this video too and shared it many times.

Engage

Social media is made for engagement. Start a conversation! Create a video that gives your audience the opportunity to share their thoughts and ideas.

Your content doesn't have to be all business. Mix it up and have fun with your videos! For example, I created a video asking my viewers which Disney character best represents them. I explained that I saw myself in Anna of Arendelle from "Frozen" because she started off naive about the world, got into a bad relationship, set off on a big adventure, came out the other end as a much stronger person, and she loves her family fiercely. The short video was viewed by thousands of people, and the answers that came in created great dialogue!

My favourite response was, "Cinderella because I'm forced to clean up after my kids!"

I feel the same way. There's a never-ending mess at my place too!

Inspire

Motivational and inspirational videos are valuable because they make people feel something. Emotion leads to action. Inspiring stories can encourage viewers to rethink their perceptions, support a cause, or buy a product. These videos can start a dialogue.

Encouraged by my fellow female entrepreneurs, I shot a video in a single take about finding my purpose again after leaving my career as a news broadcaster. Sharing my personal thoughts about how I felt like I was washed up after stepping away from my job for several years to raise a family was hard. I went on to explain how launching my own business gave me a renewed purpose and flexibility. The point of the video was to give hope to anyone going through a turning point in their life. I was nervous to post it, but the overwhelming response moved me and blew me away:

> "Beautiful and inspiring!! Thank you for sharing your heart and your journey with us."
>
> "What a beautiful journey Felicia! Thanks for sharing your heart and now you get to help others share theirs too!"
>
> "You are an inspiration to so many people around you! Thank you for being vulnerable and sharing your heart. We love you."
>
> "You are so amazing. Thank you for sharing your story. I cannot believe how similar your story is to mine. Whoa!"

Ahhh! I love my followers so much! Share an inspiring story about yourself and you may be surprised at the impact it has on your viewers. Better yet, your inspirational content may help turn your followers into diehard fans and potential clients.

Promote

Your content strategy should include posts that promote yourself and others from time to time. A common mistake that content creators make is promoting their product or service too often or, on the flip side, not promoting enough. Your followers may love what you do and what you stand for, but if they don't know about what you're offering they won't know how to work with you. On the other hand, if all you do is sell, sell, sell – you could be turning off a lot of potential customers. Sharing posts from people you care about is a simple way to promote them. It doesn't take much effort, and I can guarantee that they will appreciate the kind gesture.

You may be inspired to put more effort into a promotional post. I was. I brought my camera gear with me during the photoshoot for this book. I shot behind-the-scenes footage of each stage of the shoot, from the hair and makeup application to the multiple wardrobe changes, and ended it with the photographer directing me in front of her lens. To tell the story about the photoshoot, I interviewed the photographer, Laurie Brown, and I recorded clips of myself. The finished video promoted both the book and Laurie's photography business. She loved the video and shared it on her own account. In Chapter 2: Bring Out the Best You I explained that it's important to find your cheerleaders, but it's also important to be a cheerleader for others too!

VIDEO EXERCISE ON FINDING YOUR VIDEO STYLE

The best way to improve is to work on something that needs improving. From your Story Recipe collection that you made in Chapter 3, pick one story that you'd like to share in an on-camera video and then decide which of the following video styles would work best to tell your story:

- One spot talk
- Walk and talk
- Demonstration
- Co-hosting
- Interview

As you pick the story, and think about how you'll package it, consider the value it has for your audience. Will the video serve to educate, entertain, engage, inspire and/or promote?

- ❑ Educate
- ❑ Entertain
- ❑ Engage
- ❑ Inspire
- ❑ Promote

If it checks off one or more boxes, you get the green light to start recording.

When you publish your video, please tag me @reelawesomeproductions on Instagram or TikTok or send a link of your video to hello@reelawesome.com with the subject line: "Video style." I'd love to watch it!

PRODUCING LIKE A PRO

A lot of effort and time goes into making videos. There are steps you can take to increase your productivity and broaden your audience. They include:

- Batching
- Subtitling and captioning
- Scheduling posts
- Repurposing content

Batching content

Life is busy. Building your dream business or career, finishing client projects, and taking care of the people who matter most to you can leave your hands full and head spinning most days.

Question: How on earth can you find time to produce and publish videos consistently when you have bigger fish to fry?

Answer: Batching.

Batching is the act of completing similar tasks all at once, instead of switching between different ones, in order to boost productivity. For example, instead of checking emails throughout the day and each time a new notification pops up, choose a few set times every day to go through your inbox. Batching videos involves planning ahead and shooting several videos in a row.

Imagine how much time you'll save when you only have to do things once – the hair and makeup, setting up the equipment and the studio – instead of repeating the process every time you want to shoot a single video.

Shooting a single video each time you feel like it works, but it doesn't use your precious time wisely. Batching is smart, and I bet you'll agree once you get the hang of it.

Five steps to batch videos:

1. Write down a list of video ideas and then pick as many as you have time to tackle at once.
2. Plan the outline for each video (remember from Chapter 1: P.R.E.P. for Success to think of designing videos with a message in a similar way as eating an ice cream cone).
3. Gather different outfits for different videos if you don't want to wear the same clothes in each one.
4. Schedule a shooting day to record all of the videos you chose within the time allotted.
5. Schedule time to edit your videos and save them to your phone or another safe space so you can post them when you want.

You'll also be able to create simpler and shorter videos in less time than complex ones that involve more camera angles and more intensive editing. My best record has been nine videos shot in two hours. It's not a competition, but it is an opportunity to create a lot of content in less time so you have more time to do other things. Think about what styles of video that you want to create while you're in the planning stages. Batching content is both a time-saver and a life-saver. When you have a lot on your plate, having a supply of finished videos saves you from burnout and helps you show up for your audience come rain or shine. You can do it, and when you do – you'll be thankful you did.

Subtitling and captioning

Adding text to video is one of the best ways to engage a broader audience. A lot of people keep the audio turned off when they're scrolling through videos and would rather read than listen. And viewers who are hearing-impaired will appreciate the added text.

Subtitles include dialogue, but don't include non-speech elements such as sound effects. Subtitles translate video dialogue into other languages as well, so that people all over the world can watch videos without needing to understand the original language they were recorded in. They're also great for allowing people who speak your native language to get the gist of what you're saying without the volume turned on.

Captions are different from subtitles, and are meant for viewers who are hearing-impaired. Captions include dialogue, sound effects, and non-speech elements.

Text can be added to videos manually, or through auto-generation tools. These tools are built directly into many social media platforms and video editing programs. If one of your core values is inclusivity, captioning your videos is an excellent way to connect with more people in your audience. Go to **reelawesome.com/dontstayasecret** to see the auto-generation tools that I use to add subtitles to my videos.

Scheduling posts

Say goodbye to the last-minute scramble and hello to strategic storytelling. Scheduling content in a calendar allows you to visualize your game plan. Posting sporadically can only get you so far.

When you post content consistently, it gives your audience a sense of when to expect new content from you while building trust and connection. By mapping out your content, you'll avoid dry spells in posting and lulls in engagement. By planning ahead, you'll also be able to slip in real-time updates and important time-sensitive events and product or service launches.

Daily, weekly, monthly, or yearly – it's up to you to decide how far in advance you plan.

Consider these questions as you plan ahead:

- What events and launches are planned for specific days that I can promote?
- How much content do I need to fill my content schedule?
- What kinds of content can I create ahead of time?
- When can I batch my content?
- Are there any major events such as holidays or cultural events happening on specific dates that I can include in my storytelling strategy?
- Can I repurpose my content on other platforms that I use?
- Do I have older content that has been well-received that can be freshened up and repurposed on the same social platform?

Scheduling boosts consistency and:

Success comes on the heels of consistency.

Repurposing content

Give your videos more than one shot to reach people by repurposing content. As discussed in Chapter 1: P.R.E.P. for Success, some of the videos you make can be turned into a different format such as a blog post. You can also repurpose your videos by posting them on more social media platforms to reach different audiences. Avoid potential burnout and get the most out of the content you make.

VIDEO EXERCISE ON BATCHING VIDEOS

Batching videos is a game-changer when you schedule your posts because you'll have plenty of content to work with. This challenge will help you create 2-3 videos that you can incorporate into your social media posting schedule. It's often easier to shoot more content when you plan to record short-form videos.

Step 1: **Select a shooting day** – Choose a date where you will have a chunk of uninterrupted time to work. Give yourself at least one hour to record 2-3 videos within that time frame.

Step 2: **Prep for your videos** – Write the outlines for each of your videos and rehearse what you'll say.

Step 3: **Set up for success** – On shooting day, get camera-ready, set aside different outfits, and set up your studio and camera gear using the P.R.E.P. for Success method.

Step 4: **Record in a row** – If you're unable to finish shooting every video that you set out to do, don't worry, you can continue the next batching day. The act of recording fresh content is a win in itself!

Step 5: **Edit** – Editing a bunch of videos at once saves time. But that's not always possible, and breaking editing up is sometimes much needed for your vision and your mental health. Do what works best for you.

If you've done your best to finish this exercise, awesome job! You're well on your way to producing videos like a pro! If you're a really busy person, it's super important to get used to batching videos so you can make the best use of your time.

There are many styles of video and content to choose from. Try experimenting to see what styles gel with you. Don't be afraid to post your work, even when it's not your best. Ask for feedback. Your audience will help you figure out what they like and what they want more of. Much of what we've discussed so far has focused on creating pre-recorded videos. But what happens when your audience is watching you in real-time and expects you to lead them? That's what we'll cover next.

AFTON BRAZZONI ON THE POWER OF STORYTELLING IN CONTENT MARKETING

When I asked the founder of Scribe National, Afton Brazzoni, if I could get her insight on storytelling in marketing for this book, she said "I'd love to! I live and breathe this stuff!" Her content marketing studio is fueled by it. She and her team use a story-based approach to help companies build connections between their brands and audiences. There's a big appetite for this approach because it's so valuable and effective. Afton's experience and background in marketing, communications, and journalism helped to make Scribe National a six-figure company within its first year. I hired Scribe National to help me nail down my written brand personality after launching my own company, so you can trust that I believe in Afton's insight, and I'm thrilled to share it with you.

The most inviting and powerful way to sell products or services boils down to storytelling. While sales pitches can feel cold and uninviting if they're not highly personalized to the recipient, stories are warm and welcoming because they're relatable by nature. Stories can evoke powerful emotions – and emotion drives action. Afton says if you want to stand out in your market, tell stories. "As a business owner, being able to tell a compelling story allows you to share what you're about and what your values are." When done right, storytelling lets your audience see behind the curtain – building trust and ultimately a relationship with them – and building relationships is what successful businesses and individuals do.

Afton shares three powerful questions to consider when you plan content:

1. Who is this content for?
2. What is the purpose of the content?
3. What is the message you want to get across?

The goal with this process is to understand the who, the why, and the what for each piece of content you create. Understanding your target audience is the starting point. Are you creating content for new followers, people who have been following you for a while, or existing customers? Remember to create specific content for these three different stages of followers. Afton says by filling all three buckets, you won't leave any member of your audience out.

Once you decide what you want your audience to know through this piece of content, this becomes your message. Jot this pro-tip down or highlight it: Speak directly to the person you're speaking to. Remove the "I" and "me" in your message and flip it to "you". This concept has been introduced earlier in Chapter 1: P.R.E.P. for Success, but it's worth another mention because it's effective.

Don't be afraid to repeat yourself. You probably have several key messages, and you should be sharing them often. Studies show that your audience needs to hear a marketing message 5-7 times before they'll take action.

Always be useful to your audience. Research what stories would be helpful for your audience. Putting together videos that educate viewers on what you're all about and showing how clients will benefit from working with you is part of a solid content strategy. You're sharing, not directly selling, and people are much more open to that.

You can learn more about Afton and Scribe National at scribenational.ca.

Chapter 5
HOW TO LIGHT UP A ROOM

"You can speak well if your tongue can deliver the message of your heart."

– John Ford

Connecting in real-time with others through video conferencing is getting easier all the time. Video calls have many benefits: they cut down on travel time, travel expenses, and gives us an opportunity to meet people from all over the globe without stepping out of our own home. And we can stay in our sweatpants or pajama bottoms without anyone knowing! Woot woot! I live in stretchy pants while working from home. The downsides include unstable internet connections, dropped audio, frozen video, and worst of all, being unable to interact with others face-to-face. When you practice with proven methods from this chapter, you too will be a pro at delivering talks on virtual stages and teaching live audiences online. You'll also learn ways to keep the people interested in what you're saying, even when they aren't physically there with you.

"Welcome to the first-ever Video Confidence Academy!" Saying those eight words to my students felt like a dream, and more specifically a dream come true.

For a long time, I had imagined creating my own group course to teach big-hearted entrepreneurs and professionals how to create their own professional-looking videos using only their phone, while empowering them with the tools to look and feel confident on camera. This course would be different from the full-service videography I was already offering to clients. I admired entrepreneurs in my community who were launching group courses. They inspired me to let go of fear and doubt and be brave enough to go after my goals. I love teaching this stuff and I'm good at it, so putting my time and energy behind developing my first-ever group course in 2021 was a no-brainer. With COVID-19 restrictions making it difficult to meet face-to-face, the decision to teach the course virtually was an easy one.

When you have a solid game plan to create a new product or service, a big no-no is to drop the ball when it comes to marketing it. One of the ways I marketed the Video Confidence Academy group course was by doing multiple live interviews hosted virtually by different entrepreneurs about the power of video storytelling. This gave me a great opportunity to get to know some new people while talking about my upcoming course to each of their unique audiences. One person even signed up for my course after watching one of my live interviews. Success! Even though that result didn't happen every time I was interviewed live, I still provided value to new audiences and spread the word about what I could offer. Never underestimate the marketing potential of speaking to new audiences. People can get to know you better when you share your story, and that's one of the first steps in deciding whether they want to work with you or buy from you.

Even though I was a super shy kid, you wouldn't know it when I was in front of an audience. It was the only time I was getting the attention I wanted from my peers. My first emceeing gig was for a Christmas play at school when I was about nine-years-old. When I was 11, I volunteered to deliver school announcements over the office intercom. And I later transitioned from being an amateur to a professional presenter because, in part, I actively sought out speaking opportunities and got plenty of practice and feedback from audience members.

Seizing speaking opportunities is invaluable in growing your confidence and experience. Speaking on stages was once reserved for experts and professionals. Thanks to the ever-growing consumption of social media and the COVID-19 pandemic, the floodgates have opened to allow anyone with a message to speak to a live audience. Opportunities are just a click away if you love public speaking (and even if you don't), if you want to teach online or you dream of spreading your message to a larger audience! In this chapter, I'll teach you how you can become more confident delivering your message to a live audience.

THE SIX Ps FOR A POWERFUL PRESENTATION

Everything in the section "Preparing Your Voice and Body" in Chapter 2 is relevant and worth reviewing when you're getting ready to present to a live audience.

And these are my six keys, which all start with Ps, to create an impactful message:

1. Purpose
2. Passion
3. Posture
4. Pause
5. Practice
6. Positive

P is for **Purpose**

What is the point of your message? Nailing down how your presentation helps and serves your audience makes it meaningful and interesting for them. Make it about *them,* not you. Doing this takes a lot of the pressure off you.

P is for **Passion**

What about your topic sparks joy in your heart? Your audience can sense when you're passionate about what you're talking about. You'll automatically be more magnetic and energetic when you're passionate. Personal stories that illustrate the points of your message make it more compelling. And it's easier to be passionate about your presentation when you're familiar with the material.

P is for **Posture**

You'll look and sound more confident when you have good posture. That means sitting or standing up straight.

P is for **Pause**

You may feel like rushing through your presentation to get it over with. Instead, remember to pause and breathe. Take control of the situation and your message. It's a privilege to be able to share your message with an audience, so don't miss an opportunity to do it justice.

P is for **Practice**

Rehearse until you feel comfortable sharing your material. Once you become so familiar with what you're going to say, you can focus on being authentic and conversational. Practice in front of a mirror or record it. Then rehearse your presentation in front of a friend or family member to get their feedback so you can improve. Confidence is being prepared. Remember that we all think we sound or look funny on video, but other people are not judging you as harshly as you may be judging yourself.

P is for **Positive**

Before and during your presentation, think of a successful outcome. When you start off on a positive note, there's a far better chance it will end this way. When you bring a positive attitude, it'll be easier to remember to smile, and that simple expression helps to build trust with your audience.

A simple way to remember the six points is to keep in mind this sentence:

To pack a powerful punch in your presentation – hit the six Ps.

HOW TO SHOW YOU CARE DURING A VIRTUAL TALK OR TEACHING

People can get information instantly online, but they still show up for virtual meetings, presentations, and classes because of the need for social connection and getting their information from a trusted source.

When you have an opportunity to magnify your message with others – do a happy dance! It's honestly an honour! People are recognizing you have something valuable to share. If you ever feel resentful about having to deliver a talk or teaching, flip the script:

It's not "I *have* to do this" but "I *get* to do this!"

Thinking this way can help transform an obligation into a golden opportunity. I first shared this mindset shift in Chapter 2: Bring Out the Best You, but it bears repeating.

There are several things that you can do to show your audience that you care:

Be familiar with the video communication program

Do a run-through ahead of time so you know where important program features and functions are during a live session. This may include knowing how to turn on your microphone and camera, muting guest microphones, sharing screens, and recording the session. Understanding the program ahead of time will make your whole talk or teaching more professional and run smoother. Tell your guests exactly where they can find you with a direct link to the scheduled event.

Or, if you will be broadcasting live on a mobile-only platform, let them know they have to be on a specific app to join.

Set up your studio space

Before the live event starts, make sure you're set up in a quiet and well-lit area. Use additional lighting if you need it. Leave a good impression with a tidy and simple background so that you're the on-screen focus. The space you choose should have a reliable internet connection to avoid any video disruptions on your end.

Remove distractions

You want to show your audience that you're completely invested in them during your time together. One of the best ways to do that is to make sure incoming messages, calls, and notifications on your phone are turned off or at least silenced. This is important when you're hosting an event on a desktop computer or using your phone itself for the live broadcast.

Show up on time

I get it. It's tempting to squeeze in a few more tasks before hopping onto a video conference call. But expect the unexpected. Plan for technical issues to get in the way of a smooth start and join earlier than the planned start time. I'm not proud to admit that I've been late for a few virtual meetings because my internet connection was being lousy or the video program wasn't loading properly. It's hard to convey confidence when you're scrambling last-minute.

Give yourself enough time to set up and feel comfortable before guests show up, especially when you're the one hosting.

Go over the ground rules

Lay out the expectations and etiquette at the beginning of the event. This includes asking guests to eliminate distractions, and to keep their microphones on mute until it's their turn to speak and asking people to keep their cameras turned on because you want to see their faces or turned off when seeing each other isn't important.

Be mindful of the time

Whether you're coaching one person, or a group, or giving a talk, it's important to stick to the time limit. Talking way past the deadline shows you don't respect other people's time and that's unprofessional. If you're going to go over the time limit, acknowledge that you'll be taking longer than expected, and give people who need to leave the opportunity to exit the meeting.

Speak up and speak clearly

You don't have to buy a special microphone to communicate clearly on a virtual stage. What you do need to do is speak loud enough so people can hear you, and slow down enough so those listening can understand what you're saying.

Eye contact

One of my greatest tips for presenting live to an in-person crowd is to make eye contact with all corners of the room to hold the audience's attention. If you only look at one person or one spot for the entire presentation, the rest of the room will feel left out.

Presenting a talk or teaching a class over a video call is different than doing it in person. It's tempting to want to look at all the faces watching you on the screen. Resist the urge to scan your screen when you talk. As we learned in Chapter 2: Bring Out the Best You – the lens is your friend.

When you're sharing something important, lift your gaze and focus on the camera lens. When you do this, your viewers will see you directly looking at them. I know. It's super hard when you can't look at the people you're speaking to, but it makes a difference to the people watching you. Place a sticker or a sticky note by the lens to remind yourself to look at the lens when you talk.

It's still important to read visual cues from your audience. The best time to glance at the faces on your screen is when someone else is speaking.

Be engaging

Get your audience interested in what you're talking about by getting them involved. Do this by asking questions, doing polls, or having fun exercises that illustrate the point you're making. People feel more included and a part of your talk when they are pulled into it with you. The point of the talk is to help them, and the best way to help them is to keep them engaged!

Dress appropriately

What you wear says a lot about you. Don't let your clothing speak negatively about you. Dress the part (at least from the waist up). When you look like you take care of yourself, it gives the impression that you take pride in what you do. The next chapter will cover styling tips in greater detail.

STAYING ON TRACK

One of the biggest differences between giving a live talk in person and virtually is the interaction with the audience. In online meetings, you may look up and think some attendees look like they're in the witness protection program. When people go into hiding and show you their black screens instead of their faces, your mind starts wandering and wondering what those people are doing and if they're interested in what you're saying. Guests can get easily distracted because they're in their own homes. When audience members look away, and don't pay attention, it can really mess with your head. This is why using "The Six Ps for a Powerful Presentation" is very important. Stay calm and rely on your practice and passion to get you through moments when you're doubting yourself.

As a perfectionist, I strive to deliver a flawless presentation. But after embarrassing myself in front of a live audience as a speaker, I know that added pressure on myself isn't worth it. If you stumble on a word, or two, or four, don't stress about it. Never playback the mistakes in your mind during your live presentation.

That stress will snowball with enough weight to crush your confidence and presence while you're delivering a presentation. I've done that and it sucks. Let it go, and if you need to correct what you said, do it and keep going. You're human. Mistakes happen and, on the bright side, mess-ups can also make you appear more relatable and authentic to your audience.

Acknowledge distractions in the background to your group. For example, my girls have pulled on my sleeve to ask me for help during live coaching sessions. While this doesn't happen often, I've told my students that I would need a moment to help my girls and returned to the lesson as soon as I could. Everyone was okay with the disruption because I acknowledged it. Explain what's going on. Most people will be understanding. Those who aren't probably aren't the people you want to connect with anyways. Ignoring the distractions leaves your audience in the dark. Instead, keep them in the loop.

HARNESSING THE POWER OF SMALL LIVESTREAMS FOR BIG IMPACT

Going live isn't limited to delivering big talks or teaching on Zoom. There are other ways to build a personal relationship with your target audience using smaller live broadcasts on social media platforms. You can let your personality shine during raw, unedited livestreams, and those watching can feel like they're taking part in a genuine conversation.

Having a plan can be the difference between hosting a live broadcast that's a flop and one that's fantastic. To help stay focused and on track, jot down a few points that you'll cover and keep them close by so you can refer to them while livestreaming. The secret to becoming confident doing live presentations is to talk about what you know well.

If you like how a live broadcast turned out after it's over, remember to save, and publish it so more people can view it at their convenience. One of the great benefits of hosting live interviews or being a live interview guest is that you get exposed to a new audience and that can lead to new followers.

Presenting to a live audience may seem intimidating and risky at first; much like walking a tightrope without a safety net. However, when you prepare using "The Six Ps for a Powerful Presentation" along with taking steps to show your guests that you care, you'll light up any room – in person or online. Instead of putting pressure on yourself to give a flawless presentation, aim to be yourself and to help those who are looking for it. So, before you speak into the microphone, remind yourself:

You don't have to be perfect, but please be present.

This is a principle I stick to when I go live. While I absolutely love speaking to an audience in person, teaching students virtually has given me flexibility to make a living doing what I love while spending more time with the people I love most. And that's what it's all about.

VIDEO EXERCISE TO BOOST YOUR CONFIDENCE GOING LIVE

Growing confident in your abilities to go live in front of an audience can be learned. If you haven't tried broadcasting live before, and you need some support, ask a trusted friend to go live with you. If you'd prefer to go solo, plan your message and practice what you want to say before going live.

Here are some ideas to boost your confidence with a live broadcast:

- Co-host a talk with a good friend about a topic you have insight on.
- Host an interview and provide questions or talking points to your guest ahead of time.
- Do a "show and tell" featuring your products or services.
- Plan a series of live talks covering common questions you get from your audience.
- Teach your audience something in your wheelhouse.

The common thread that weaves all the above ideas together is they all involve you talking about something you're comfortable with. When you know a lot about a topic, you'll be able to speak confidently about it.

The best way to become confident in presenting live is to start presenting live, and keep presenting live. Going live will help you break out of your shell, so you don't stay a secret. With that in mind, pick one of the above ideas that I suggested and do a live broadcast. You can do it!

Don't worry about the number of people watching. Instead, focus on the message and the value you're bringing to your audience.

After going live, ask yourself "How did it feel? Was I proud? Nervous? Did anything surprise me? What did I do really well during the live? What will I have to work on for next time?" Write down your experience so you can review it down the road and see how far you've come in broadcasting live.

____

____

____

____

____

Once you've completed your first live broadcast from the list, choose another idea and go live again! I'm so proud of you for having the courage to step out of your comfort zone, and for sharing your message and your special gift with others.

LYNDSIE BARRIE ON FACILITATING VIRTUAL GROUPS AND DISCUSSIONS

Before Lyndsie Barrie became my friend and mentor, I only knew of her from her Instagram posts as the founder of YYC Fempreneurs – a community of female business owners in the Calgary area. It was December 2020. I had just launched my business, Reel Awesome Productions, and realized I could really use help marketing it. I had been following Lyndsie online for a little while, and I saw that she was planning a virtual leadership and marketing conference in January. I signed up at no charge, and with no strings attached and not knowing what to expect, and what I got was useful information from different speakers. More importantly I developed amazing connections with female entrepreneurs, including connecting with Lyndsie herself.

After the conference, I joined Lyndsie's signature Fempreneur Marketing School. Lyndsie started the online school in 2019 after several women asked her how to market themselves on social media. She loved the opportunity to connect like-minded women with each other as well as the convenience of teaching online: "As long as you show up and you care about people, not all of it has to be mind-blowing. You bring them something of value, that's all that matters to them. And they don't have to find a babysitter and drive their car to a location."

If you want to create a group training program, take Lyndsie's advice: "Don't build things hoping people will come. If you value your time, you don't want to build a course that no one wants to sign up for."

Fempreneur Marketing School began as a free six-week course. Instead of planning exactly what she would teach each week before launching it, she took the guesswork out of what her students would want and asked for direct feedback to make it irresistible for them. Lyndsie says you don't have to build a product or service before you market it:

> "Put out good enough and ask for feedback instead. Whether you're making a product or service, you know that type of person you love working with. Talk to that person. When you're building something for them, such as a group online session, get ideas from them. It's okay not to have the whole plan. You just need to show them that you care and that you're open to building it as you go."

More than 170 women have graduated from her marketing school with the confidence and connections they need to succeed in business, including me.

Lyndsie is a master at creating a supportive community among women by giving them a platform to share their wins and to learn from each other. These are her four keys to engaging people during a virtual group discussion:

1. **Have a niche audience –** Everyone in the room should be there to achieve similar goals.
2. **Get them talking by asking them meaningful questions –** Try to ask your guests or students prompting questions that relate to everyone in the room.

Lyndsie's examples of effective questions to ask group members are:

What has your experience been trying to achieve _______?
What were the barriers you faced?
What were things that worked?
What is your number one goal now?

3. **Steer people towards positive discussions –** If someone is bringing the whole group down, you probably don't want that person in your group anyways. Don't be afraid to respectfully shut down negativity. Boundaries are important.
4. **Be a good listener** – When it comes to facilitating discussions, trust that the right thing to say will come from what someone else is talking about. Acknowledge what they are saying to show you care.

Using these techniques creates community and engagement within the group and takes some of the pressure off you to do all the talking.

Sometimes things don't go smoothly. When everything in a video call seems to be going badly – chill out. It may seem counterintuitive not to freak out when there's technical trouble, but Lyndsie swears by it: "If you're doing your best, and the more chill you are, the more your audience will roll with it."

Lyndsie's easy-going nature lets her to roll with the punches when things don't go as planned, but one thing she doesn't budge on is sticking to the schedule.

We know that going over the time promised is disrespectful, but as Lyndsie points out, it also doesn't give off an image of success: "It looks like you don't have anywhere else to be. You want to look busy and like your time is valuable."

If self-doubt is stopping you from creating a course, or hosting a workshop, Lyndsie reminds us that you don't have to be a seasoned professional to run a successful online program – you just need to care and do your best.

You can learn more about Lyndsie at yycfempreneurs.com.

NOREEN MUSIC ON PRESENTING ON VIRTUAL STAGES

If you've ever watched Noreen Music speak in front of a crowd, you'd know she's a seasoned pro. Noreen's been at it for more than 30 years and she's fantastic at it. Noreen captivates audiences with her professional and conversational style. In her former corporate career, she learned how to speak to different audiences – at art unveilings, rental tenant meetings, to the media, you name it – she's probably done it. Now she gets behind the microphone as a professional organizer and productivity coach: "It's a great way to convey your message and get to know people and have them get to know you."

While Noreen prefers speaking to audiences in person, she's been able to share her message with people all over the world through an abundance of online opportunities due to the COVID-19 pandemic: "It's given me more opportunity to reach a broader audience. I have met coaches and speakers and people that I would never have met otherwise. It's just opened up my eyes to other people and business opportunities. The more I speak the more people know who I am and what I do."

If you want to speak on stages, Noreen's sharing her best advice with you: "Develop one signature talk." These are Noreen's top three tips to narrow down your focus to create that one signature talk:

1. **Figure out that one topic you're confident in talking about** – Keep it simple and stick to one thing you know very well.

2. **Go deep on the topic and not wide** – For example, instead of covering 12 points, cover 3 points in more depth.
3. **Explain the *why* and save the *how*** – In other words, discuss why the topic is important in the presentation, and save the technical talk for separate teachings such as workshops.

With a wealth of knowledge and experience, Noreen has developed two signature talks: "How to Get and Stay Organized at Home" and "Five Keys to Overcome Productivity Overwhelm." After delivering these talks in person and online, Noreen has learned a speaker has to work harder when everyone's not in the same physical space. Part of it is screen fatigue. To combat this, she recommends designing virtual talks and teachings to be the following lengths:

- 30-45 minute talk including a question and answer session at the end
- 60-90 minute webinar/training session because people are more prepared to learn

Make the time you have with an audience count and, while you're there, have fun with them! These are some of Noreen's secrets to engaging an audience:

- Ask them lots of questions.
- Use polls.
- Give real life examples and stories because people learn more from stories than facts.

We all start somewhere. Noreen encourages budding speakers to gain more exposure by offering their talks to different groups, such as local libraries and churches. You may not get paid, but you'll gain valuable speaking experience and networking opportunities.

When you want to light up a room, take yourself out of the spotlight and aim that spotlight on your audience. Noreen says when the purpose of the talk is to serve others and not yourself, it takes the weight off your shoulders and gives you freedom to be yourself: "You have something very important to say. We all have lessons and stories and things that the world needs to hear. So, your message is important. Your message is critical to get out to people."

You can learn more about Noreen at organizemyspacecalgary.com.

Chapter 6
CAMERA-READY SECRETS

"You never get a second chance to make a first impression."
– Will Rogers

My panties were falling on live TV.

"Is this seriously happening?" My mind raced. "NOT NOW!"

It's 6:59 am. The floor director's belting out the countdown to get my attention. Rushing from my desk to my marked spot in front of the camera to open the morning show at 7:00 am had become a daily ritual, but this time something was wrong – terribly wrong. Normally, when anchoring the news, I'm laser-focused on bringing each story to life with the proper tone and emotion, but because my underwear was slipping from the weight of the microphone pack clipped onto it, all I could think was "Please stay up. PLEASE STAY UP! CURSE YOU GRAVITY!"

My wardrobe choice for the day was a dress. Wearing a dress during a live broadcast is usually not an issue because you can hide the microphone pack under it by putting on a compression thigh sleeve or attaching it to the top of stockings.

Heck, you could even attach it to the back of a bra! But for some reason (that I can't remember), I didn't use any of these options with the specific dress I was wearing. Instead, I thought clipping it onto my stretchy hip huggers would work fine. It didn't.

The wardrobe malfunction wouldn't have been a big deal if I had sat at a desk while delivering the news. But when I was on CTV Morning Live, all the hosts and guests stood. I avoided a near disaster because of my glutes. To prevent my undies heading all the way down south, I clenched so hard you could have cracked a walnut between them! It's situations like these that I'm thankful for working out! It's a miracle they didn't end up by my ankles. THANK GOODNESS I held them up, and held it together during the show, so it didn't end up on a blooper reel. That would have been a hard one to live down.

As soon as the floor director signalled that the show was in a commercial break, I let out a huge breath. Frazzled and relieved all at once, I grabbed my slouching panty-pack combo and shuffled back to my desk. The breather gave me enough time to properly attach the microphone pack to something that wouldn't give way. I was back on track and ready to roll. Hallelujah!

I learned a very important lesson that day: dress appropriately so you can focus on your message.

It's hard to focus on doing hard things when your wardrobe's getting in the way. It's also hard for someone watching you in a video to focus on you and your message when your wardrobe isn't giving off the right message.

This chapter is about how to look camera-ready. I'll keep it *brief*. Okay, enough with the puns, but this topic is going to be short and sweet on purpose.

When I was asking my family and friends for topics to include in this book, one of the suggestions was how to look good on video. So here it is! I want to clarify that this book is about how to showcase both you and what you have to offer in the best light; it's not a book of tricks to transform you into looking like a completely different person. You are amazing and beautiful, just as you are. Your appearance is important, but it's not everything. If you're confident in the way you look on camera right now, then "High five!" and "Strut your stuff!" But if you need some pointers, you're in the right place.

Never feel like you have to look like a model or a movie star in your videos to be seen or heard. Sure, some people have won the genetic lottery. We all know someone who's hit the jackpot in the looks department. But a person's appearance is only part of the whole package. What's more important is to give people a chance to fall head over heels for you by showing them the real you.

Wearing makeup doesn't mean you're not showing people your true self. If you saw my makeup drawer, you would know that I'm a makeup addict! I happily fill in my eyebrows, draw a classic winged eyeliner along my upper lashes, and pop on some gloss before I walk out the door every day. Makeup helps me feel more put together and confident. But I've dialed my makeup routine down quite a bit from what it used to be. I used to take my sweet time getting camera-ready for my YouTube videos. Sometimes I would spend an hour or longer getting dolled up – that's time I'll never get back! On the other end of the spectrum, because of tight deadlines when I was working in TV news, I got my hair and makeup done all by myself in about seven minutes before it was time to start a live show. I know how to get the job done fast!

Most of my career has been on screen. Over the years, I've learned some amazing tips and tricks from talented stylists and professional makeup artists. And now I'm going to pass them onto you. There are three main things you have to think about to look camera-ready:

- Wardrobe
- Hair
- With makeup or without makeup

WARDROBE

What you *say* matters, and what you *wear* speaks volumes even before you open your mouth. If what you're wearing is distracting, no one is going to listen to what you're saying. When you pick out an outfit for a video ask yourself the following questions: "Is it true to my personal style? Does it express my personality? Does it give off the impression I want to make with my audience?"

For example, showing lots of skin may not gel well with your target audience. To create an image of professionalism, you may opt for more professional clothes in your videos. Of course, this rule isn't written in stone. Wear what makes you feel your best and own it! Use your style to express who you are. Be aware, though, you can only make a first impression once, so choose what you wear wisely.

If you're open to suggestions, here are three simple styling tips that can help you stand out in video:

1. **Wear solid colours** – Bright, colourful clothes pop more on camera than black and white ones. They also add more colour to your face. Try out different colours that you have in your closet to see which ones are most flattering on you. Skip colours that wash you out.
2. **Stay away from small, busy prints and patterns** – When you wear clothes with tiny prints and patterns, such as narrow stripes, it can cause strobing, which is often distracting to the person watching. Strobing happens when small patterns flicker on video. If you love to wear prints, don't fret. A better-looking option is to choose clothes with big, bold images on them.
3. **Wear jewelry that doesn't jingle or dangle** – Unless your brand is about big jewelry, keep your accessories small. More specifically, avoid jewelry that makes lots of noise when you move because that can distract from what you're saying. While big earrings certainly carry a WOW factor, save them for special occasions. When you wear jewelry that has lots of movement, viewers are drawn to the movement, which can distract from your message.

HAIR

Do you have short, medium, or long hair? Honestly, it doesn't matter.

The principle is the same for hair at any length: keep it neat.

That may mean tying up your hair to keep it off your face when you're in a video. Or applying some product to lock in the style. At the very least, run a comb through it before you hit the record button.

When I first started my broadcasting career, one of my colleagues suggested several times that I chop my long hair into a bob: "It'll make you look older, and you'll look more professional."

I gave it some thought, but I couldn't bring myself to do it. My long hair has been a large part of my identity, and I wasn't ready to part with it. So I stuck to my guns and left my long locks alone for my entire career in television news. Whether pulled back, or on my shoulders, I usually try to keep my hair neat on screen.

MAKEUP

Not everyone is comfortable wearing makeup, and that's okay. That's why I'm breaking this section into two parts:

1. With makeup
2. Without makeup

With makeup

If you're a makeup maven, you've got this section covered. But if you're someone who doesn't wear a lot of makeup and wants a few suggestions to level up your makeup, then let's get to it:

Face – Get matched with the correct shade of foundation and concealer that matches your skin tone. I've had great success using makeup brands meant for studio work. Finish with a translucent powder to remove excess shine that can look greasy on camera.

Eyebrows – Fill in your eyebrows a little darker than your natural hair colour to frame your face and to give your face more expression. Eyebrows make a big difference in how you appear on camera! My natural eyebrows are barely noticeable. So, I fill them in with a waterproof gel and eyebrow pencil to make them big and bold – just how I like them!

Eyes – Do you like mascara or eyeliner? Use what you're comfortable with. When it comes to eyeshadow, go matte. Glittery and frosted eyeshadows often have fallout, leaving you with little specks of glitter all over your face. Matte eyeshadows are flattering, no matter if you're 21 or 91.

Cheeks – If you're familiar with how to contour your face, do it! Contouring can help bring out your bone structure that can look flat in video. If that's too complicated, a simple swipe of blush on both cheeks is enough to give you a healthy glow.

Lips – Apply a lip colour after a moisturizing lip balm to avoid dry lips. Enhancing your lips with some colour will bring attention to your mouth and what you say.

The camera and lights can make you look washed out, so apply more makeup than you normally would to help you look more awake, refreshed, and expressive. If this makeup-talk is too intimidating, let's narrow it down to the three things that will make the biggest impact on screen:

1. Remove the shine on your face with translucent powder.
2. Fill in your eyebrows.
3. Apply a lip colour.

That's it. Easy-peasy.

Without makeup

You can put your best face forward on camera when you don't wear makeup. The secret is to be well-groomed and hydrated.

When you don't wear makeup, wearing bright clothing can help make you pop on screen. You'll come off as confident when your hair looks good too:

Face – When you don't have makeup on top of your skin, make sure it's clean and moisturized before hopping in front of the lens. Remove the excess shine from your face with blotting papers or with a single ply of tissue paper after pulling a sheet apart.

Lips – Apply a lip moisturizer, such as lip balm, regularly to keep your lips flake-free. Living in Calgary's dry climate, I carry lip balm with me everywhere I go. If I don't use it, my lips look like a snake shedding its skin. Ew. One important thing you can do to improve dry lips is to drink plenty of water. Not only will it keep your lips plump, but it will also do wonders for your vocal cords.

Eyebrows – If you have wild eyebrows, take a moment to tame them by running your fingers over them to help shape them. If you have extra time to tame them, shape them with facial hair scissors.

And a reminder: if you're not a fan of facial hair, remove it – either on your own or with the help of a professional.

Men

Anyone can use the tips in this chapter to look their best on screen, including men who don't typically wear makeup. If you're a guy or know a guy, the secret to looking amazing on camera is to put effort into grooming. Get a fresh haircut, shave, and moisturize. Everyone looks better when they're well-hydrated. One of the best tips I've given to men who need to show up on camera is to remove shine with either blotting papers or some powder.

No matter who you are, or what you look like, a big secret to showing your best self on camera is to:

Look the way you want to be remembered.

You do you! Think about your favourite outfit. How do you feel when you put it on? Smarter? Sexier? Dressing in a way that makes you feel confident can transform you into a more capable version of yourself on screen and off screen. It also shows your audience that you care about them because you put effort into your appearance.

In this chapter, we've covered how to outwardly improve the way you look to boost your confidence.

In the next chapter, we'll go over how being confident in who you are and what you have to offer will help you stand up to people who want to cut you down.

VIDEO EXERCISE ON PUTTING YOUR BEST FACE FORWARD

I've been using the makeup and styling tips that I've shared in this chapter for years. Use whatever feels right to you and work them into your routine when you're getting ready to go on screen.

The next time you use these tips to get camera-ready, shoot a video! You've put in the effort, so you might as well capture yourself looking your best! You can talk about anything you want in the video, but if you want an idea try the following exercise:

Introduce yourself to your audience with five interesting facts about yourself.

Some ideas for facts to talk about are:

My dream job is ________.
My dream vacation is ________.
My favourite food is ________.
My favourite book is ________.
I truly believe ________.

If you publish the video on Instagram or TikTok, please tag me @reelawesomeproductions. I can't wait to learn more about you!

LAURIE BROWN ON HOW TO GET GLOWING ON CAMERA

I want you to hold this page and quickly flip to the front cover of this book right now. Once you're done, come back.

DANG! I have to say, I look good! But I definitely never roll out of bed looking like that. It was a team effort.

I'm going to introduce you to the two amazing women who made the vision of my book cover become a reality. First up is Laurie Brown of Laurie MacBrown Photography. When I saw her work, I instantly knew she could pull off exactly what I wanted for my book.

Laurie's a portrait photographer in Calgary. She's photographed countless people of all ages. Most of her clients are mature women. In Laurie's experience, the reason women hide from the camera is because they're afraid they won't like what they see.

Laurie possesses an otherworldly talent to capture the true beauty within all of us – that some of us never knew we had. Here's what she has to say about why you should show up on camera:

> "Your future self will thank you for existing in photos. Your family and descendants will likely treasure your portraits more than you know. If self-confidence is holding you back, then I urge you even more to show up for the camera because it's the most effective way to build confidence in yourself!"

Laurie's best secret to getting camera-ready comes down to hydration:

> "Not only should you drink lots of water and avoid things that are dehydrating (like coffee and alcohol), but you should also moisturize every bit of skin the camera will see. If you do nothing else, do this. Your skin and eyes will glow, and I'll take care of the rest!"

You can learn more about Laurie Brown at lauriemacbrownphotography.com.

ADRIENNE FURRIE ON PUTTING YOUR BEST FACE FORWARD

Adrienne Furrie loves to joke that she came out of the womb with a makeup brush in her hand and dove right into her mom's makeup bag. The full-time professional makeup artist, entrepreneur, and mom of two says she's always been fascinated with the transformative power of makeup, clothes, and hair. Countless clients have experienced her magic through her work behind a makeup counter, on set, and as a makeup coach. As an entrepreneur, she's making her mark on the beauty industry. Adrienne dreamed of creating her own high-quality product line. Now she's done it. Her Canadian-made cosmetic line is focused on clean, natural ingredients. Adrienne is a true master of her craft, and sees the bigger picture of how our appearance can affect our confidence: "I think that our makeup and our clothing and hair choices can really impact how we feel, which then really impacts how we show up."

When I met Adrienne on the set of my book cover photoshoot, she instantly put me at ease after taking the time to understand the look for which I was going. I usually tread carefully working with makeup artists. It all started after a bad experience I had when I was 17. I had asked a makeup artist to do a trial of my makeup look for grad, and I ended up looking like a possessed demon with my eyelids drowning in a sea of merlot eyeshadow! I was so shocked and disappointed with what I saw. I held back tears as I stared back at my reflection in the mirror. It didn't look like me at all. She clearly didn't know how to work with the shape of my eyes.

Ever since then, I've been pretty picky with who I trust to do my makeup. Adrienne is one of the very best makeup professionals whom I've had the pleasure of working with.

Adrienne is openly sharing her best on-camera beauty secrets with us. Her pro tips are excellent additions to the ones in this chapter. Her perspective on beauty at any age is eye-opening.

While developing this book, I spoke with several women in their 50s who told me they shy away from showing up on camera because they don't look like they did in their '20s and '30s. If you've fallen into this trap, Adrienne challenges you to think differently:

> "I think we are beautiful at every stage of life, and it just changes. In our 40s we can't compare ourselves to 20-year-olds. We've got 20 more years of life experience. We've had the sun beating down in our face for 20 more years. We've earned our wrinkles. We've earned our smile lines. When we look back 20 or 30 years later, we'll think, *oh my gosh, if only I'd really appreciated how beautiful I was then.* It's so easy to look at, especially people in their teens and their 20s, and see them just radiating energy, health and vitality. But you know, when you're 50, you're gonna look back at your 40-year-old pictures and be like, "Oh my god, I'm an idiot for not recognizing how beautiful I was." When you're 80 and you look back at that young spring chicken 60-year-old self, you're gonna think, "What was I complaining about? I was a total babe!"

Amen Adrienne. Amen.

She says there's not a ton of differences between the makeup that younger women should use compared to mature women, and not just for on-camera use but in general. The biggest difference is in the product texture. Adrienne recommends older women use more cream-based products such as cream blush and liquid foundation and concealer to give the appearance of more youthful-looking skin. Stay away from strictly powder foundation on the entire face, which can emphasize dry skin and wrinkles. Younger people can get away with heavy matte foundation and powder because their skin is smoother. Adrienne points out that using coloured powders is different than strategically using a colourless translucent powder because translucent powder helps manage shine and works well at any age.

As we get on in years, our eyebrows usually lose fullness and colour. Sometimes they become thinner because of over-waxing or over-plucking earlier in life. Take the time to define them with a product such as a brow powder.

When it comes to lips, a good choice for older women are products in a lighter shade with shine, such as a gloss which reflects light, because lips lose volume with age.

Here are Adrienne's beauty tips that work for women at any stage of life:

Lips

If you're someone who always ends up with lipstick on your teeth, avoid wearing a bright red lipstick right before hopping on a video call because you'll probably end up with lipstick on your pearly whites.

If you were born with thin lips, a good tip is to stick with lighter shades such as a light pink. Use a lip product that has some gloss to help your lips look a bit fuller.

With or without makeup, get in the habit of using lip balm regularly, not only when you're going on camera. It's a little thing you can do to help your lips stay plump.

Skin

Give your skin a good buff before going on camera. Use something to gently exfoliate such as a face cloth. After buffing your skin, Adrienne recommends applying a light moisturizer on your face and any other body parts that will be visible on camera. This is especially helpful if you have darker skin, which can look ashy when it's dry.

Highlighter

While highlighter and dewy skin may look lovely in person, be intentional with how you use highlighter. Too much highlighter can reflect too much light and cause a "whiteout" effect when strong lighting is used for video or photos.

Nails

Aim for nice-looking nails. If you like nail polish, paint them. Fix chipped nails and worn-out nail polish. Otherwise keep them short and clean.

Teeth

You can whiten your teeth, but it's not necessary. Instead, getting your teeth professionally cleaned every six months will make a big difference in your smile.

Hair

Maintain your hairstyle. If you have short hair, make sure it's freshly cut. If you colour your hair, get a root touchup if necessary. And before you go on camera, play around with your hair to figure out what looks best.

Adrienne's a firm believer in portraying yourself the same way in photos and videos as you do in person: "We need to be showing up as who we are. I'm always very careful when I'm doing hair and makeup for someone that's getting branding photos done. I ask, 'How much makeup do you normally wear? How do you normally look?' Because we don't want you to look so radically different online. If you normally show up as quite a glamorous person, then that's great. But that's not everyone. So, if that's not an authentic way for you to show up in your real life, don't put all this extra pressure on yourself to look like a radically different person because that's not going to work. Ultimately, you're going to feel really out of alignment with the final result." Adrienne and I took this into consideration for my book cover images. I love getting glammed up and the look on my front cover isn't far off from how I'd show up to a fancy party!

Making at least some effort to look camera-ready is important. Adrienne says feeling good about what you see can just take little things that stack up to make a final image that we feel comfortable with. You want to have positive feelings about the image that you see being reflected back to you. Getting camera-ready, says Adrienne, doesn't have to be complicated: "Don't let it get overwhelming. Pick one or two things that you feel confident putting your energy into."

You can learn more about Adrienne at adriennefurrie.com.

Chapter 7
OVERCOMING CRITICISM AND CRICKETS

"A rejection is nothing more than a necessary step in the pursuit of success."

– Bo Bennett

"So why, then, given all of the dreadful story's obvious flaws, is the thing an award-winner? Well, something had to win." You probably wouldn't bat an eye if you were reading this review about a random story from a published magazine, but I imagine you'd feel very different if it were aimed at your work. I didn't make that review up. The author of an article delivered a crushing blow as he ripped apart a television feature that I poured my heart into. Like you, I care about what I put out into the world. So, when others don't see it the way you do it can suck big time. The author didn't stop there. I'll explain more later, but let's just say he called my work a fancy piece of crap.

I hate to admit it, but I also care about the number of likes I get on social media. Why do I care what others think of me? Turns out I'm a grown woman who struggles with the need for outside validation. The performance of each of my personal and professional posts matters to me. Whenever my phone starts buzzing, I often give into the urge to check it.

I know I'm not alone, because there's an underlying behavioural science to why I care. Research shows social media platforms such as Facebook, Snapchat and TikTok use the same neural circuitry that is caused by gambling and recreational drugs to keep users on their sites for as long as possible. When a post gets a like or share – Cha-ching! Instant gratification, and immediate cravings for more. Scientists have compared social media interactions to a syringe of dopamine being injected straight into the brain. Dopamine is a chemical produced by our brains that plays a big role in motivating behaviour. It gets released after we exercise, have sex, taste something so good that it makes us do a happy dance, and when we have successful social interactions. This pleasure rush rewards us for beneficial behaviours and motivates us to do them again.

Have you seen *The Social Dilemma*? It's a 2020 docudrama exploring the dangerous human impact of social networking. Knowing that tech experts have designed apps with the power to manipulate people and governments while nurturing addiction makes my skin crawl. Experts in the film explain that the popular apps most of us use every day are intentionally designed to be highly addictive to keep you on them for as long as possible so they can expose you to more targeted ads. After finishing the movie, I immediately turned off all social media notifications. But staying notification-free didn't last long. With a need to stay connected to market my own business through social media, I've flipped the switch back on for some apps. If there's another free way to find leads, make sales, and build a community without social media, please let me know. My mental health will thank you for it.

Until then, my emotions will continue to hop on a kiddy rollercoaster ride whenever the "cha-chings" come in slowly or don't come in at all.

FIELDING CRITICISM

I've learned from the women whom I've coached that one of the greatest roadblocks that's stopping them from hitting the publish button is fearing the negative feedback they could get once their video is out in the public. I get it. It's one thing to post a picture of your product or service, but publishing a video with your voice and face starring in it makes it a lot more personal and places you in a vulnerable position.

Do you ever focus on negative things while discounting the many positive things said about you, or the amazing feats you've done? That's negative filtering. It's common and most of us do it from time to time – I'm guilty as charged. As a perfectionist, I gravitate towards what I excel in; I run away from what I don't. But I've learned it's better to:

Aim for progress, not perfection.

When I was anchoring the news at different stations, I would receive really nice compliments from loyal viewers about my work – the kind that gives you warm fuzzies and makes you say "Aww" out loud:

"You're the best news anchor."

"I love watching you on TV."

"You're my favourite."

It feels so nice being someone's favourite! On the other end of the spectrum, though, when someone sent a negative review it would throw me off and I would obsess about how I was right and how I should or could try to change the viewer's mind.

While I was working at CTV Regina, the co-anchors loved to talk about the Saskatchewan Roughriders. They would make small talk about the CFL football team with me during the broadcast while I was filling in as the weather specialist. Unlike the entire newsroom – and the rest of the province – my blood didn't bleed green. I couldn't fake it. It's not that I don't like the Riders. I'm just not a huge football fan. A viewer didn't hold back in his email – an email that everyone in the newsroom could read: "Felicia wouldn't know what a football was if it hit her straight in the face." "Ouch," I winced, "You had to choose the face. Thanks buddy." That comment was a sucker punch to my ego. "I'm such a nice person", I said trying to console myself. "How could this guy not like me? If he met me, he wouldn't think that way." As much as having the superpower to manipulate thoughts would come in handy, it wouldn't work all the time. Select viewers feel entitled to tell you exactly why they don't like you, and nothing you say will change their mind. In other words:

Haters gonna hate.

I had to learn to let mean-spirited comments go. Sometimes you can't change someone's mind, and you shouldn't feel like you have to do it. I was going heavy on the negative filtering, which is often tied to unrealistically high expectations of yourself. If you're a perfectionist like me, perfection is the gold standard that everything must meet. Everything else isn't good enough. If you fall short, it can mean forgetting all of your past successes and focusing on the few times that you didn't reach that ridiculously high bar.

The internet is packed with people you don't know. There are people who won't hold back their strong opinions. There are people who have different expectations because they were raised under different circumstances than you. There are people who are unwell. Criticism comes with the territory when you're making content. You may face it early on, or when you get more eyeballs on your work. Focus on making videos that you're proud of instead of what someone could say or did say to drive you.

Have you ever watched a celebrity respond to a mean tweet? It's a guilty pleasure for millions. That's why *Celebrities Read Mean Tweets* is a recurring segment on American late-night talk show *Jimmy Kimmel Live*. The hate the stars get is often jaw-dropping and uncomfortably amusing. For example, Halle Berry read this tweet from someone who misspelled her last name: "Halle Barrie's boobs are lopsided." The American actor snapped back: "Well, when they're real, that happens." Maisie Williams read this tweet: "Maisie Williams looks like a very young grandma." The *Game of Thrones* star didn't say a word, but the hurt on her face was heartbreaking.

Haters are harsh. It sounds bad, but truthfully it's kind of comforting to know that even gorgeous Hollywood A-listers get burned. To some degree you finish these types of video clips feeling better about yourself. Watching videos where people are criticized creates a sense of community, drawing a thick line between US and THEM. It also serves as a form of group therapy for celebrities who know they're not the only ones being bullied. Hearing the insults brings out the mama bear in me: "Who has the nerve to say something so cruel like that? What's wrong with them? They deserve more than a time out!" Haters will go out of their way to bring darkness to those who shine. If that ever happens to you, never let them dim your light.

> "I learned long ago, never to wrestle with a pig. You get dirty, and besides, the pig likes it."
>
> – George Bernard Shaw

Online trolls are the thorn in the side of civil internet users. When certain people can hide behind their digital devices, they go out of their way to get ugly. While it's instinctual to want to defend ourselves from their online abuse, engaging them is usually futile and counterproductive. The Center for Countering Digital Hate recommends against feeding the trolls. There are times when standing up against a bully matters and makes a difference. The way you respond also matters. Take the high road. But trolls are playing a completely different game. While we may think engaging trolls and debating with them is a battle of ideas, trolls don't necessarily care about winning or losing.

They want their ideas to be heard by as many people as possible. Don't give them the time or attention that legitimizes and spreads their hateful thoughts. When a troll is under your skin and all you want to do is rip them a new one, keep this in mind:

Don't feed the trolls.

There have been at least two times where comments from bullies really hurt me: once when I was working in Regina and the other was when I was working in Halifax. While the emails were sent at different times by different people, they both said similar things: "The only reason Felicia was hired was for racial balance." My mind flew into defence mode, "Um, wow – WOW, in the worst possible way." It's true that I was the only Asian television personality at the time at both these news stations. But I have figuratively and literally shed blood, sweat, and tears to earn my positions – and reading that someone thought the only reason I was there was to check off a diversity box made my blood boil – twice!

Clenching my teeth as my fingers furiously typed away on the keyboard, I respectfully responded to one of those emails and explained that I was proud of my heritage. I thought it would put an end to his cruel intentions. Gosh, was I wrong! The man shot back with another nasty email about how my ethnic background wasn't the issue. He didn't hold back when he said I was terrible on TV, and made it clear that he was very well educated and graduated from prestigious schools so his opinion was more important than mine. Engaging with him was such a waste of time. Lesson learned: Never respond to a mean comment when you're angry or emotional.

If a troll comes knocking on your digital door, don't answer it – and leave the door locked. For the love of all things good and holy – don't feed the trolls!

My face has made it on the cover of a magazine, not once, but several times. Hold the polite applause – I didn't end up in the magazine because I'm hot stuff. This particular magazine features scandals and gossip. Eight years after these two issues were published and in select grocery stores, I dusted them off and read the articles again to include my experience with criticism in this book. One of the issues featured an article titled "What's a nice girl like Felicia Yap doing at an awards dinner like this?" In a nutshell, the author took a cheap shot at the feature story that I researched, wrote, and produced about centenarians – a fancy word for people living over 100 years old – that won a regional 2012 *RTDNA Adrienne Clarkson Award* for showcasing diversity in a story. The author said: "It's a turd, but it's a turd sporting a monocle and twirling a walking stick." "Yikes!" My eyes grew wide in horror as I digested what I had just read. My inner voice got defensive, "Come on! A turd with a monocle? That's one fancy piece of crap." The author's creative use of imagery was impressive and offensive at the same time. I didn't know whether to laugh or cry. He finished the article with "But listen, I don't want you to hold this thing against poor Felicia. She's so excited about it . . . I won't burst her bubble if you won't. After all, she seems like such a nice girl." If it's not obvious, the author wrote the article without any of my input.

My heart sank all the way to my gut the very first time I read that article. It was a slap in the face. Hands shaking, I wanted to throw the whole magazine in the trash. But I stopped myself and packed it away in a box. Eight years have passed since I first read the article, and going over it again unearthed old feelings of inadequacy and unworthiness. As a public figure, I've had to develop a thick layer of skin to repel naysayers and trolls. Bestselling author Simone Elkeles said it best: "Opinions are like assholes, everybody's got one and everyone thinks everyone else's stinks." Even so, a super stinky comment still cuts right through my armour and pierces me where it counts. Winning that award has been one of the highlights of my career in journalism. When someone says something negative about you, resist the urge to run away from it. Assess if there's some truth to the comment, and if you can correct it the next time. Figure out what the intention of the comment is, and if it's coming from the right place to make you better. In this case, the motivation wasn't to help me improve – the tone of the article was callous. The author is entitled to his opinion, and while he clearly didn't like my story I'm not going to let his opinion that he made public strip the joy from this accomplishment. It wasn't solely my win. It was a team effort and a team win. I had an awesome group of camera operators, editors, and producers that helped me with the story.

I'm not saying this is the case for that author, but I think sometimes people go out of their way to be cruel because *hurt people hurt people*. For certain people who have been emotionally, mentally, or physically wounded, intentionally hurting others behind the shield of their computer screen is a safe way to lash out.

In case you're wondering why I bought the magazines – I wanted them as keepsakes. I'm an ordinary person who will probably never make it to the cover of a scandal magazine again (fingers crossed). I'm glad I kept them because now I get to write about it and I've realized:

When someone is smack-talking about you,
it's because you're doing something big.
So the next time you feel hated on, celebrate it!

REFLECTION EXERCISE ON HANDLING THE FEAR OF CRITICISM

Being criticized is uncomfortable. Stepping out of your comfort zone and in front of a camera puts you in a vulnerable position. Answer the following questions to help take control of your fears of posting videos so it's not so scary anymore:

What's the worst thing that could happen if you get a negative comment on your video post?

___

Review what you've jotted down. How likely do you think this terrible thing might actually happen?

___

If it were to happen, what are the steps you would take to rebound?

___

___

On the flip side, what's the best thing that could happen if you post videos of yourself?

___

___

Think about a specific experience where you felt rejected or criticized. What positive things came from this experience? What lessons did you learn?

___

___

HEARING CRICKETS

> "Take criticism seriously, but not personally."
> – Hillary Clinton

It's one thing to hear negative feedback about a post, but another one that stings perhaps almost as much is hearing nothing at all. Receiving little to no response following a post that you worked really hard on is disappointing. When you've spent time and effort to create something that you think is great and that doesn't align with the response you think you're going to get, it can be a huge letdown.

I find it easier to post about my business on my professional social media accounts than on my personal ones. When I was promoting my YouTube channel, I shared links to my DIY videos on my personal Facebook account. Initially the response from my family and friends was strong. I felt so loved and supported. They were excited for my new endeavour as a YouTuber. But over time, as I posted more DIY projects, interest waned. I got very few likes and shares. I felt like the people who know me personally didn't care and that hurt. However, over time, I've realized that my DIY content isn't for everyone. No one should be expected or obligated to watch and hit the like button on what they don't want to view. While I believed in the quality of work I was producing, I was sharing the right content with the wrong audience.

Maybe some of your close family and friends aren't the wrong audience – they simply haven't warmed up to you in your new role or identity. There's a solid chance that they've watched you grow up and don't see you as an expert or leader – yet. They may still see you as the quiet kid, or the girl who struggled in school, because that's their most vivid memory of you. They haven't seen everything you've done to step into your power. One of the best ways to shake them up and wake them up, though, is to share – not just once, but often. Be bold and share your wins and your losses. So while there's a part of me that's reluctant to update what I'm doing professionally with my nearest and dearest, giving them repeated glimpses of what I'm up to helps them warm up to the idea that I'm taking charge and doing cool new things.

We all start somewhere. Having a small following on social media doesn't mean your content isn't valuable or worthy of attention. Be patient. The right-fit people haven't discovered you yet! Having an intimate community provides an amazing opportunity to nurture relationships. It also means having a more forgiving audience.

When I was first gaining experience on the anchor desk in a small news station, I made a lot of embarrassing mistakes. Thankfully the newscasts were pre-recorded, allowing myself and the production team to do a couple retakes if necessary. The ability to redo a line after a flub was a security blanket. But one newscast in particular showed me that the blanket wasn't completely secure. While we started the program like we did every day, the director in the control room who produced the show experienced technical issues during one segment. Although my delivery was smooth, we had to reshoot the segment three times because of technical problems. On the fourth attempt, I made a mistake and asked to do it again.

We did and finished the newscast. I eagerly watched the lunch hour broadcast on TV like I typically did. But this time, instead of a professional delivery, I saw myself on the television screen announcing, with a laugh, "I screwed up. Let's do it again." I froze. "Oh my goodness!" I blurted in disbelief. "Did that just happen?" That gaffe had not been taken out. Maybe crawling under my desk in the fetal position would help me brace against what was to come. I started sinking in my chair when the director burst out of the control room and into the newsroom and apologized. I couldn't be angry. All was quickly forgiven. This slip-up was an anomaly for the director who consistently put out amazing work. Mistakes happen. I was more worried about the fallout from my blunder. I waited for rude comments from viewers to come rolling in. And you know what? No one called the station. No one wrote a nasty email. I bounced back quickly from this embarrassment because of a very forgiving smaller audience.

Keeping a close eye on follower or subscriber numbers can feel like being the Good Shepherd. Even losing one may send you on a mental search to understand why they went astray. But I want to tell you to let that lamb go. When there's a little dip in your follower and subscriber count, please don't get discouraged. We all want our number of supporters to organically grow. It means you're doing something right. But losing followers doesn't necessarily mean the opposite. A person may unfollow because their situation has changed, and your message doesn't resonate with them anymore. It's not always about you.

I'm not going to create perfect videos all the time. I'm not perfect. No one is. Some critics may hate my work and call it a fancy piece of poop – but I'm not going to let their words make me feel like one. There's a transformative difference between taking things personally and professionally. Taking criticism or crickets to heart means it's a personal struggle for you. It's hard to jump back in the saddle and stay the course when you take things personally. When you realize it's part of the process, however, your mind reframes negative feedback and rejection as small bumps in the road that won't stop you from reaching your goals. That is the benefit of taking things professionally. Above all:

Listen to your heart and not the bullies.

VIDEO EXERCISE ON EDITING TWO CLIPS TOGETHER

Learning how to edit well develops in a step-by-step progression. You've learned how to trim clips in the "Video Exercise on Trimming a Video Clip" in Chapter 1. Now we're going to build on that skill by joining two clips together.

In this exercise, I'm going to ask you to shoot two separate video clips of yourself. This is a great chance to use one of your ideas for a video! But if you need inspiration, you can use one of the following ideas:

1. If you're comfortable sharing a personal story, use your response to the last questions in the "Exercise on Handling the Fear of Negative Feedback" from earlier in this chapter to explain an experience where you felt rejected or criticized in the first clip. In the second clip explain what positive things came from this experience.
2. If you'd like to keep it professional, talk about one myth or misconception you face in your industry in the first clip. In the second clip, describe what is the reality.

Capture the two separate videos of yourself using two different backgrounds. You don't have to go far to get a different background. To help you change the framing of your next shot, try moving the camera a few steps left or right or further or closer to you.

Shooting with two different backgrounds allows you to avoid a jump cut. A jump cut happens when you have two back-to-back shots with an exact or similar camera set up, but the subject is in two different positions because the continuous action in between them is missing. It can happen when an unwanted clip of someone talking is removed, leaving two clips that don't exactly line up side-by-side on the editing timeline.

Once you're happy with your two separate clips, open a new project in your video editing program. At the time I wrote this book, joining two clips together had to be done on a video editing program.

Select your two best clips in the order you want them to appear and add them to the timeline.

If you need a refresher on how to trim clips with an app that you downloaded, review the video exercise in Chapter 1. Trim each of your clips so that only what you want stays on the timeline. The two clips should butt up against each other, side-by-side on the timeline. When you press play, the two clips should play consecutively and seamlessly without any flashes of black between them. Save the finished video to your phone.

You're ready to publish. Way to go!

To see what video editing program I recommend, and to watch a tutorial of how to join two clips together, go to **reelawesome.com/dontstayasecret.**

Please show me your video by tagging me on Instagram or on TikTok @reelawesomeproductions. I can't wait to see your work!

YVONNE CHAPMAN ON FACING REJECTION

Getting a single "No" when you're really counting on a "Yes" is painful. But what would hearing "No" hundreds of times feel like? While facing rejection after rejection could make many want to pack up and turn the other way, my cousin, Canadian actor Yvonne Chapman, has faced the lows head on. With grit and determination she has nurtured a career that's brighter than ever. Yvonne has landed big roles in big productions. She has starred as Mina Lee in the reboot of the iconic Canadian TV series *Street Legal* by CBC, and was cast as the villain Zhilan in The CW Television Network's reimagining of *Kung Fu,* an American action-adventure television series, and has brought Avatar Kyoshi to life in Netflix's *Avatar: The Last Airbender.*

To put rejection in perspective, Yvonne says when you look at her history of acting roles on IMDB there are so many more roles that she auditioned for and didn't land. When she isn't working on a television production, Yvonne estimates she auditions for an average of two roles a week. "Rejection is just a part of the game," adds Yvonne, and even though facing rejection at the beginning of her career was emotionally and mentally taxing she's learned to recalibrate her mindset. And once she experienced helping indie films cast their projects, Yvonne gained a whole new perspective of what it's like to sit on the other side of the table. She views rejection differently now. Understanding that the majority of people watching are supportive, and are on your side, eased the anxiety and hurt from getting told "No":

"Knowing that people want you to succeed helps to take away that fear. That nervous energy is always going to be there a little bit because we care about what we do, but don't let that cripple you."

Although she says she was happy with her finance job, Yvonne left that nine-to-five gig to pursue acting full time in 2015. Her ease and confidence in front of the camera started developing nine years earlier when she started modelling professionally. Yvonne's love for acting runs deep in her bones and in her blood. Her grandmother was an actor in Asia. Yvonne says she loves acting because she gets to jump into so many kinds of lives, and it gives her the ability to see a different perspective of life from the viewpoint of the different characters she plays.

Yvonne explains the fear of the unknown can really get under your skin and stop you from pursuing your passion: "The fear of the thing itself is always *greater than the thing*. Once you make the unknown *known*, it has less power over you." When I asked her about how to handle negative feedback and fears about posting videos, Yvonne reminded me that there is more positivity than negativity in the world: "Sometimes you do get super self-conscious about putting yourself out there, but more often than not people are quite supportive." An important part of her strategy to stay positive while producing work for the public is to ignore negative feedback that's harmful. Instead, she focuses on paying attention to constructive criticism that helps her to become better. Yvonne admits that knowing the difference between what can help and what doesn't help is a process. Being afraid of rejection and negative feedback is normal, but Yvonne says, "You don't need to feed it. That's a huge thing for me. Don't feed whatever you don't want to grow."

That's brilliant! Think of it as depriving certain cancer cells of nutrients so they starve to death instead of reproducing.

If you're looking for more tools to gain confidence on camera, Yvonne's got it right:

Don't feed what you don't want to grow.

Burn that one into your memory. Yvonne's perspective is valuable because she's used to being a public figure. Her insight is trustworthy because I know she'll be completely honest with me. From playing with Barbies as kids to bad breakups with partners, we've supported each other in our personal and professional journeys. I have seen the sacrifices Yvonne has made to chase her dreams, and I couldn't be prouder. Not only can Yvonne act, she's an amazing teacher as well. I've been lucky enough to take some acting classes under her direction. I can't wait to see where her talent and positive attitude takes her next.

You can learn more about Yvonne on Instagram by following her at @ypchapman.

Chapter 8
YOU ARE THE REAL DEAL

"Experience tells you what to do;
confidence allows you to do it."
– Stan Smith

Ever felt so scared that you couldn't do something because you believed you weren't good enough? It didn't matter that you conquered past projects and gained valuable experience, because in your head it happened by luck and not by your talent or qualifications. The self-doubt creeps in and twists your stomach up in knots because you're scared that the imposter police will hunt you down and arrest you for posing as the real deal.

Been there. Done that. Let me explain.

By 2013 I had been working as a broadcast journalist for five years, covering countless stories in the Prairies and in the Maritimes. I had been the late-night anchor and weather specialist for the weekend news on CTV Atlantic for a couple years. I was used to presenting the weather for Nova Scotia, New Brunswick, and Prince Edward Island for both the late-night and the supper hour newscasts. After producing and anchoring hundreds of newscasts in that role, I was itching for a new challenge and praying fervently for it. That opportunity came when I least expected it.

Following a late-night shift, I finally drifted off to sleep at 1 a.m. A mere four hour later, a vibrating sound kept poking at me, repeatedly, until my eyes flew open and my heart raced as I realized it was my phone.

"Hello?" I mumbled as my lips struggled to work together.

"Hi Felicia. We need your help filling in for the weather right away." The frantic voice explained one of the co-hosts was sick and couldn't go to work. The live show would be starting in two hours. I snapped out of my sleep-induced daze.

"WHAT? ME? NOW?"

The exhausted part of me wanted to stay in bed. But the deeper, hungry part of me took charge – this was my chance to try something new with a new audience! Also, I couldn't let the team down. Television news works as a well-oiled machine. When one part is missing or broken, someone will step up to replace it so the whole system can keep running. And boy, did I run that morning.

"I'll be there as soon as I can!"

My pounding heart slammed my chest wall as I ran to the washroom. Splashing my face with icy water and fumbling for my jar of moisturizer. I threw on a bright outfit to stand out on screen, zoomed out the door, keys in hand, and bolted into my car.

Sitting behind the wheel for a moment, I caught my breath and told myself I could do this: "You'll be okay, you'll be okay."

But as I started driving, my mind started racing: "Can I pull this off? I'm not a trained meteorologist. What if I look like a bona fide idiot delivering the weather for this show I have never done before?"

My heels flew over pebbles and pavement as I sprinted through the parking lot and burst through the station's back doors. After taking a deep breath to compose myself, I sat down at my desk and started with what I knew how to do – gathering information online about the weather in different cities and towns. As I entered the information into the computer, I quickly learned there were several important differences between presenting the weather on the shows I had worked on compared to the one I was about to do. The morning show included the weather for all four Atlantic provinces, while the rest of the shows I had worked on included three. The weather maps that I had to present included different places and the order of the slides were different than what I was used to. I felt incredible pressure to get everything right on my first try. To stay calm I reassured myself that while the setup was different the fundamentals of producing a weather presentation were the same. For the most part, I knew what I was doing. For the other parts, I relied on a great production assistant who was very familiar with the morning show.

Live TV is like a train barreling down a track. You need to lay the pieces of track before it arrives. It's not patient. It won't wait for you to be ready, or perfect. It keeps thundering ahead towards the deadline. The floor director signalled that the time to prepare was up. "Ready or not," I said under my breath, "here I come!" I was leaning heavily on the NOT side, but I had to let go of my fears – it was show time! I put on my bravest face and brightest smile, walked under the intense studio lights and co-hosted a two-hour morning show – that I had never been trained to do before – while presenting new-to-me weather updates throughout the program.

The floor director signalled the countdown with his hands, *10-9-8-7-6-5-4-3-2-1.* All clear! The train left the station. Phew! I had made it! I didn't do anything super embarrassing to make it onto a blooper reel. And it actually went really well!

During the whole show my mind was screaming "YOU DON'T KNOW WHAT YOU'RE DOING" – but I managed to stay cool and collected on screen. In my case, it wouldn't have been possible without the amazing people behind the scenes who work hard every day to deliver the news. Teamwork really does make the dream work. The biggest takeaway from this experience was:

A pressure cooker forces you to face the heat, but that's when you find out what you're really made of.

I went home relieved. The weight lifted off my shoulders and I succumbed to an afternoon nap. As a night owl, I returned to sleeping after midnight. Then history repeated itself. My phone buzzed. I glanced at the time: 5 a.m.

"Can you fill in for the weather again?"

"Sure." I said half-asleep.

We would repeat this cycle several more times that week. Each time that I was called to fill in was a surprise. Each time I may not have felt qualified, but I dove in anyway. Each time I was more ready than the last. But I soon found out my body and mind couldn't keep up.

It hit me when I least expected it. I was finished for the day and leaving the station when suddenly it felt like my heart was gripped by a noose with a grenade attached. This had never happened to me before.

Each painful breath gave life to scary thoughts that my heart could burst. I held onto the hood of my parked white Toyota Corolla for support. I carefully inhaled short, shallow breaths – anything deeper could have pulled the pin and then it'd be GAME OVER.

"Please God, don't let me have a heart attack in this parking lot!" I pleaded. "I don't want to end up on the evening news for this. What's happening to me?" Thankfully, after ten minutes, the pain subsided. The fear that something was wrong didn't.

I confided in the producer of the morning show about what happened.

"I think it was a panic attack," she said.

"Panic attack?" I said scratching my head. "But it happened after I finished my job, when the stress was over!"

A quick check online confirmed her suspicions were correct. Panic attacks often appear suddenly without an obvious trigger and usually ease after a few minutes. *Check.* The person having a panic attack may have a sudden fear they will die. *Check.* These attacks cause you to worry about the possibility of having another one at any time. *Check.* You could have stuck a big fat "FRAUD" label on my forehead, and I wouldn't feel the need to take it off.

FEELING LIKE A FRAUD

Doubting your abilities and feeling like a fraud is known as imposter syndrome. Psychologists Pauline Rose Clance and Suzanne Imes first studied it in the 1970s and coined it as the "Impostor Phenomenon." They found it occurs among high achievers who are unable to internalize and accept their success.

Does this hit close to home? If so, you're not alone. Roughly 70% of people experience these feelings at some point of their lives. While it was initially thought to only affect professional women, research has shown it affects a wide range of people and not just women. You don't have to be highly successful to be affected by it. Studies have shown that people who have imposter syndrome can get their work done, but if they keep feeling this way for a long time it can lead to depression and anxiety. Almost everyone feels like an imposter sometimes – especially when we set near-impossible standards for ourselves. But never let those feelings control your life for so long that it stops you from recognizing your worth and your abilities. It's taken me a while to understand this, and here's what I've realized:

You're more capable than your fears would have you believe.

Scribble it on your mirror. Say it out loud. Memorize it. While saying "Yes" to presenting the weather on the morning show had me shaking in my heels, it also allowed me to high kick a big, beautiful door open. It didn't happen overnight. When seeds are planted, good things can take time to grow. I returned to my regular shift on the weekend news. I wasn't panicking anymore, but the intense feeling of wanting something greater for myself refused to retreat.

Several weeks later, one of the main TV hosts at the station announced that she was leaving for another career. So, the internal reshuffling of on-air personalities within the newsroom began.

Getting her job would be a longshot. She was a co-host for an evening-hour flagship program with decades of experience.

"What's the worst that could happen if I show I'm interested?" I asked myself. I couldn't see any downsides, so I applied for her job with the hope that it would show those in charge I was ready for a change. Action is the fastest path to clarity. There were several applicants for the job, but I knew I had to make a move or stay unfulfilled in my current position.

The day came when I got called into the news director's office. He bluntly told me I wouldn't get that job. "Damn!" I thought as my heart tightened. While I braced for another letdown something amazing and unexpected happened.

"We're promoting you to anchor and co-host CTV Morning Live. You'll also be anchoring the news at noon."

My eyes grew wide. My jaw dropped. My last name may be Yap, but for a moment I was speechless.

"Y-y-yes! I'll do it! Thank you. THANK YOU!"

It turns out my repeated appearances on the morning show impressed the people in charge of hiring. It's amazing what can happen when you have the courage to step out of your comfort zone. I walked out of that office feeling like I hit the jackpot, not only for what it would do for my career but also for its impact on one of my most important relationships.

I called Andrew to tell him the great news. He was thrilled! Nurturing a long-distance relationship with wildly different schedules was tough. While we were in an exclusive relationship, we spent almost all of it apart – living in different cities to pursue our dreams. When he was off on the weekends from medical school, I was working the weekend shift. This new job would mean I would work weekdays. This new job gave us the chance to finally line up our lives!

REFLECTION EXERCISE ON IMPOSTER SYNDROME

What part of your life do you feel most like an imposter?

Why do you think that and what evidence do you have to justify it? My guess is, there will be none.

What are you really proud of that you've done, created, or experienced in that area of your life? Focus on the positive.

What does success in that area of your life look like?

What mistakes have you made in that area?

What lessons have you learned that can help you take action?

Being a perfectionist means you strive to be the best. Recognize that making mistakes is okay. Create a new story about yourself. Be aware of the story you tell yourself when you're in a situation that triggers imposter syndrome. What will you say to yourself when imposter syndrome hits?

What steps can you take to build your confidence in this area?

VIDEO EXERCISE ON IMPOSTER SYNDROME

Because many of us experience imposter syndrome at some point, it's a great topic to cover in a video. Connect with and encourage your viewers by creating one of the two following short-form video ideas:

Video idea 1

Shoot your first clip by saying:

"I sometimes feel like an imposter because ________. But here's what I say to myself when imposter syndrome strikes."

Next, shoot the second clip with your answer to the question. Use different backgrounds when shooting the two clips to make the finished product visually exciting and by using different backgrounds you can help avoid a jump cut.

Edit the two clips together. If you need a refresher on how to do it, please refer to the "Video Exercise on Editing Two Clips Together" in Chapter 7.

Video idea 2

Create engagement with your audience by asking questions and getting their feedback. You'll only need to record one clip for this idea.

Here's an example of what you can say in the video:

"Have you ever felt like an imposter? I've felt like a fraud when_________. What do you say to yourself when imposter syndrome strikes? Share your answer in the comments."

Challenge yourself to shoot your clips in one take. Once you're happy with the video, post it. If you publish it on Instagram or TikTok, please tag me with my handle @reelawesomeproductions so I can cheer you on!

TO LOVE AND BE LOVED

"Inaction breeds doubt and fear.
Action breeds confidence and courage."
– Dale Carnegie

For more than seven years I dedicated my energy, time, and talent to improving my skills as a news anchor, producer, writer, interviewer and co-host. I would regularly study recordings of my own newscasts, and every night watch several other newscasts with anchors I admired to see how I could improve. As a perfectionist who wanted to create the best, I gave it my all every day to get the job done right. It meant getting up in the wee hours of the morning, staying late at work to prepare for the next day, and sometimes setting up interviews ahead of time at home on my own time. I started my new role without any formal training. It was a very steep learning curve at the beginning, and I stumbled many times climbing it. My mess-ups were broadcast live to thousands of homes.

Once, a senior reporter noticed I wasn't presenting the change in the price of gasoline correctly and called me out on it with his booming voice. I'm so thankful he did. While I was equally embarrassed and mortified that I had been repeating the same mistake for a while, I learned how to do it the right way and never made that error again. It's okay to mess up once in a while because:

Mistakes have the power to make you a better version of yourself. Humility allows it to happen.

My last day at CTV Atlantic, which I didn't know at the time would be my last day working in the news, was emotional. My final words on the air were: "I'm Felicia Yap. From our CTV family to yours, thank you so much for watching." The newsroom erupted in applause all at once after my final signoff. I looked around the newsroom in disbelief and in wonder. Love and gratitude swelled inside me. I couldn't hold back the tears. These people whom I had so much love and respect for were giving me a standing ovation! One of life's greatest gifts is to love and be loved in return. I learned so much and gained so much experience working in that newsroom during those five years. I entered the doors as a stranger, but I walked out with a family of lifelong friends and a full heart.

After I packed away my belongings, my boss sat down with me in his office and showed me the results from the latest ratings period. I held my breath, hoping for the best. TV sweeps periods are both an exciting and anxious time for people working in the industry. The results act as a report card of the programs that viewers love and the ones they skip over. Ratings can lead to firings, promotions, and cancellations. "The promotions team will be sad to lose you because they won't be able to get as much for ads once you're gone," said my boss. The noon show that I had poured my heart and soul into as the anchor and producer had the highest jump in ratings compared to all the other shows at the station! This was a BIG WIN! When I took over the noon show, it was underrated. When I left, it was unstoppable! I had big dreams to turn the small show into something great. Adding fresh features to the newscast such as interviews, live hits with reporters, and packing it with new local content made it something special.

While I led this show, none of it would have been possible without the reporters and dedicated team of camera operators, editors, and producers working hard behind the scenes.

DROP THE DOUBT

I love telling stories – but this book almost didn't exist. You wouldn't be reading these words if I let my insecurities get the best of me.

When my marketing coach, Lyndsie approached me with the idea that I should write a book, I politely told her I'd think about it. But my own destructive thoughts immediately shut it down: "HELL NO! Who would want to read my book? I'm a nobody. I don't have anything good to say! I can't run a business, take care of my little girls and write a book! It's not possible."

But soon after, a renegade voice pulled away from the pack and started speaking up: "Wait! I do have something important to share! My story matters, and it will matter to somebody. If it's important enough, I will find a way to make it happen!"

That encouraging voice was getting louder, and I was listening. Thoughts about writing a book were keeping me up at night. I knew I had to act on it otherwise I'd feel stuck – and sleep deprived.

Lyndsie planted a seed, and over a few days – and mostly sleepless nights – I nurtured that seed with positive thoughts about sharing my triumphs, challenges, and knowledge to help others accelerate their confidence on camera. A desire to empower people to achieve their dreams was activated within me.

I finally stopped questioning myself and my abilities. "Do I want to do it? Can I do it?" faded when I realized that I had a moral obligation to share what I know with the people who need my help. It was no longer a "HELL NO!" – it was a "HELL YES!" I decided to drop the doubt and dive right in!

I hopped on an emotional rollercoaster when I signed up to write this book. I've laughed, I've cried, I've doubted my ability to write something valuable, and I've felt guilty about all the time I've spent writing and not with my little girls. Much of the typing happened in the wee hours of the morning with sleepy eyes that hadn't fully peeled open. And when my eyes were beyond ready to shut after my kids had gone to bed, I continued to sit in front of my computer thinking and writing.

The reason I kept running towards the finish line, even when I saw the tape move farther and farther back, is remembering that I would be helping someone, and that someone is YOU!

Once I made up my mind that quitting was off the table, I simply kept going.

It takes a village, and this book wouldn't be possible without an amazing support system who have taken care of my daughters without question so I could write, coached me through the writing process, and cheered me on all the way until the thoughts in my head had been printed on paper.

Many people wish they were confident without taking action. To gain confidence in whatever area you're focusing on – do the work. Change your behaviour and build your confidence muscle. Flex my friend, flex! Above all, never discount your experience, talent, and your heart because:

You are the real deal.

EMILY CHASE ON HOW CREATING VIDEOS CHANGED HER LIFE

You have the potential to open up many doors for yourself when you make video creation a priority. My dear friend, Emily Chase is a shining example of this. We met at a party in 2010 while our partners were in their first year of medical school together and instantly clicked. We quickly bonded over a love of fashion, and, as we've matured, being moms. Emily even called her social media accounts "Shopping Soulmate" after one of our shopping trips together. Prescribe her and I a round of retail therapy together and it's guaranteed we'll instantly feel better!

Emily is an influencer and is proud of it. Emily has taken steps every day to earn that title – and one of the most effective ways she's been able to achieve this is by showing up in video daily. I interviewed her for this book because Emily is a genuine example of how showing up consistently on social media has changed her life for the better. She started with a blog, but soon realized it wasn't working for her and her busy lifestyle as a new mom. Then she launched her Instagram account in October 2019 as a way to promote her business as a digital artist. During the pandemic of 2020, she decided to include her passion for fashion, so Shopping Soulmate also became a styling, lifestyle brand. By engaging with her audience through video storytelling, her following grew to more than a thousand Instagram followers in about a year.

Creativity runs through Emily's veins. She studied fashion design for goodness sake! Like many of us, limiting beliefs froze her from pursuing what burned in her heart.

She believed she wasn't good enough to take her passion seriously. For many years, because her husband is a doctor, Emily was surrounded by overachieving medical students and doctors who were more excited to talk about patient symptoms instead of what made her excited, such as painting and style. She walked away from that important part of herself for at least six years: "Putting it away felt like a part of me was hibernating. Like I wasn't a whole person, and I was always a little sad because I know there was a part of me that I wasn't honouring." But a change of scenery sparked that dormant flame.

She and her family packed up their lives and moved from Saint John, New Brunswick, to Ottawa, Ontario, for her husband's residency training. While living in Canada's capital, Emily joined the non-profit organization Art for Mental Health, which raises awareness of mental health and the importance of art as treatment. As a creative woman living with anxiety, it's a cause close to Emily's heart. Emily created several paintings for the group's fundraising event, and her friend convinced her to appear on camera to show the world that she was the face behind her artwork. When the media learned about their initiative, the non-profit was invited to talk about the fundraiser. Emily stepped out of her comfort zone and became the speaker for the organization.

Even though she was terrified, she eventually gathered enough courage to record her first video about a new iPad cover she bought because it felt like drawing on paper – something she felt was useful for other digital artists to know about. Emily says she expected the trolls to come knocking after posting the video. To her surprise, the trolls didn't bother her. Relieved, Emily made a goal to show up once a day in video: "Slowly but surely, it gets a lot easier, and your brain starts to work with it instead of giving you anxiety."

You wouldn't think it when you watch Emily light up the screen with her magnetic personality, but she too has worked through insecurities to show up in video. She had a long hard battle with her naturally curly hair – straightening it or pulling it back into a ponytail every time she was going to shoot a video. She's now learned to love and care for her crowning glory. Emily's gorgeous golden locks are one of my many favourite things about her! Many of us often fight against our natural features that make us unique. I'm guilty of it. I still spend a lot of time and energy curling my straight hair because I think it looks better than what I was born with. Emily has also struggled with hormonal acne and scars on her face for most of her life, but she's not letting these things get in her way.

To give her an extra boost of confidence, she harnesses the power of good lighting and flattering camera angles to look her best. Emily's got it right. Good lighting and good angles make a huge difference in the way you look on screen.

If you've thought about playing around with digital filters, Emily says go for it! "If you feel like you need a filter to make you more comfortable to show up and tell your story," she says, smiling, "more power to you!" Emily uses a light filter unapologetically: "It colour corrects, you can still see my acne marks a little bit. Everything is blurred out and it makes me feel better." Choosing to use filters or to record without them is a personal choice, but I agree with Emily: if using a filter gives you the courage to create videos, do it!

Watching Emily transform from a nervous wallflower to a vibrant and engaging wildflower has made me an incredibly proud friend. She stuck to her goal to show up for her followers every day, and this ultimately led to building connections and her brand: "Honey, if you don't go on and tell them why you love it so much, why would they care?"

Exactly. You need to acknowledge posting videos of yourself is scary, at least initially. If you are scared, go on record to say that you are scared. People will relate to how you feel because they'll know you're being authentically you.

In moments where she needs an extra push to get over imposter syndrome to show up on video, Emily remembers this powerful message:

Nobody cares.

You can use this too! It's not that people don't care about you or what you have to say. As Emily explains, it means the mountain you've created for yourself isn't as big as you've made it out to be: "You're so wrapped up in your own insecurities, but so is everyone else."

Emily says she has connected with so many amazing people that she never would have met unless she took that first scary step to shoot a video of herself talking about her iPad cover: "It's changed my opinion of working with women. When we were going through fashion school, you're in competition with each other. You can't share your ideas because the other girls will steal it. Now that's such BS. I have met so many amazing women that I would have never met if I kept believing that lie. Collaboration over competition." Emily's advice for content creators just starting out is invaluable:

Know your worth and don't be afraid to tell it to other people.

Emily explains that it's more than your personal worth – it's your financial worth as well: "As an artist there's a misconception that you're willing to work for exposure." One client made her feel bad about getting paid, implying that all she wanted was money. So, she sadly worked for free. Emily says she wouldn't tolerate that now. There's a ton of work and planning involved with social media content creation: "It's a giant misconception that we are willing to work for exposure or free stuff. It's nonsense. Sometimes it means you have to turn down unpaid work. But if someone believes in your work then they will be willing to pay what you deserve." Emily's right. By standing up for your worth, you're helping others do the same for themselves.

Being an influencer is something she never dreamed of as a kid because it didn't exist when she was a kid. She always loved drawing and grew up wanting to be a fashion designer: "The fact that other people are now acknowledging it as my job and my brand, that is mind-blowing to me. People buy products because of what I share. You don't know who's watching." Emily is also proud of being an influencer: "It has changed every aspect of my life. I still can't believe how much my life has changed in a year because I showed up on my page and shared my story. It gives me more confidence in my day-to-day life, which is amazing, because if the internet has accepted me, then society should be fine!"

Setting healthy boundaries with what you share and how much of your life you decide to share online is important. Emily is clear that she doesn't show her daughter or husband in her videos. That way she knows she can spend time with her daughter and husband along with the rest of her family knowing they're not involved in the brand she's building.

When you're unsure if you should share something, ask:

Is sharing that content part of your brand?

Everyone has different comfort levels with what and how much they share. Put each piece of content you create under a stress test. If the content doesn't serve to entertain, educate, inspire, engage, or promote your brand, drop it or tweak it until it does. What you share should add value to the lives of the people watching.

Now settled with her family in Fredericton, New Brunswick – the same place she went to school for fashion design – Emily has hit her stride. She's thrilled to work with local clients that she admires. She's living her dreams as a professional personal stylist and a model.

I adore her, and so do her loyal followers. Emily is one of my greatest cheerleaders, as I am for her. While we live thousands of kilometers apart, love is greater than distance. She's an example of how taking small steps to show up for her audience has transformed her world: "If you're going to do it, do it right. Don't let it scare you because you'd be shocked by how much your life will change in a year just by showing up on camera. The camera is your friend." So, if you're thinking of growing your brand and increasing your impact through video, remember:

**When you allow yourself to just be you,
the impossible becomes possible.**

The world isn't looking for more perfectly polished people with flawless skin and impeccable oratory skills. The world is craving authenticity. People want to see people who look like them, love the same things as them, and are going through the same things as them.

You can learn more about Emily by following her on Instagram @emily.shoppingsoulmate and on TikTok @emilyshoppingsoulmate.

Closing
PUTTING THE PIECES TOGETHER

"There are no secrets to success. It is the result of preparation, hard work, and learning from failure."
– Colin Powell

Being uncomfortable helps us grow. Sometimes that means facing a present struggle head-on or, in my case, a piece of the past – I'm talking about the comment from my aunt that I described at the beginning of this book: "You're not going to make it. You're Asian. There aren't many people on TV who look like you."

What my aunt said many moons ago fueled me to work harder and smarter to prove that I'm not an exception, but rather an example of what can be done.

I knew it had to be included in this book, and I knew I had to ask for her permission to share it. As someone who doesn't like conflict, I would have much rather swept it under the rug and kept it there. But important things and hard things are often the same. I played out different scenarios in my mind: "What if she says 'No?' What if she gets upset? But what if she says 'Yes'? I'll never know unless I ask." So, I did – 14 years after she said it to me.

Turning to her I said, "You know I'm writing a book, right?"

"Yes."

She was giving me a ride home. We were alone. It was a perfect opportunity. But, getting out what I wanted to say was like pulling teeth. I stared down at my hands that were furiously rubbing together. Time was running out. We were almost at my place. "It's now or never," I thought, coaxing myself to say what I needed to say.

"A long time ago, you said I wouldn't make it on TV because I'm Asian. It was a huge reason why I worked as hard as I did. I know you meant well. Can I use it in my book?"

Without missing a beat, she replied: "Do whatever will help you tell your story."

My eyes grew wide and so did my smile.

"Thank you so much! It means a lot and it'll really help tell my story in the book."

"It's fine. It was a long time ago."

"Amazing! Bless her heart!" I thought, exhaling with relief. "That was so much easier than I thought it would be!" I wasn't sure this pivotal story would make it in this book, because I was scared of what my aunt would think of me sharing it. I'm so glad I was brave enough to ask. The mountains we create in our minds often disappear in an instant once we have the courage to be bold.

REFLECTION EXERCISE ON HOW FAR YOU'VE COME CREATING VIDEOS

Doing the work that I've asked of you in this book takes courage. It has been a pleasure to lead you on this journey. How do you feel now about showing up on camera and creating videos? Write your answer down.

____

____

____

To understand how far you've come, we need to look back at where you started. Flip to the "Reflection Exercise on How You Feel About Making Videos" in the introduction of the book and review your responses.

Has anything changed? If it has, what's different about you and how you feel about creating videos now?

____

____

____

My goal has been to guide you to a point where you've become confident both creating videos and showing up on camera. I truly hope I've helped to guide you there. It would mean a lot to me if you recorded and sent me a video about how much your confidence has grown after putting this book into practice.

Please send your video to hello@reelawesome.com with the subject line: "My video confidence journey."

Video confidence won't magically appear overnight, but it will be yours if you commit to practicing the principles and doing the work explained in this book. I've given you a detailed framework along with the tools to help you and your stories soar with video. Keep using video to put yourself out there because:

It's hard to be a success when you're a secret.

What's stopping you now? Whenever you need a refresher on a topic related to making and showing up in videos, take a look at the table of contents. You should be able to find the guidance you need to get back on track.

If you've done enough and tried your best at something, such as video editing, and you've realized that you still don't like it, find someone else to do it. Hiring someone after you've put in the work to realize it's not a good fit for you allows you to focus on what you're good at and what you love doing. Before you go that route, though, I encourage you to try the entire process of video creation so you can really appreciate each step and have the insight to hire someone who will do an excellent job for you.

If you're determined to level up your ability to create videos by yourself, I can personally teach you one-on-one how to do it. I can also coach you to present yourself confidently in front of an audience. If you enjoy learning alongside a supportive group of people, I also offer that option through my Video Confidence Academy. And if you want more guidance on starting up a social media channel or account to beef up your online presence with video, let me help you!

If you still feel stuck or want to advance your video confidence skills send me an email at hello@reelawesome.com.

Together, we can figure out what's standing in your way. We're not done yet. I'm leaving you with an exercise that will help to boost your comfort level with video batching.

VIDEO EXERCISE
FOUR-IN-ONE CHALLENGE

You're going to ramp up your video production in this challenge! The goal is shoot four videos in one day that you'll schedule to post later over the span of one week.

Review the "Five Steps to Batch Videos" section in Chapter 4 for instructions. Remember to have a total of four outfits with you on your scheduled shooting day so you'll look different in each of your videos. Once you've edited all four videos, write out the captions and save your work.

Next, decide on a week that you'll post the videos and if you'll repurpose them on different platforms. Tag me in all four videos using my handle @reelawesomeproductions on Instagram or on TikTok. You can also email me links to your videos with the subject line: "Four-in-one video challenge."

I'll verify that you've completed the challenge and send you a link to book a discovery call with me. We'll discuss what you're doing really well and any areas that could use some improvement. I can't wait to hear from you!

I hope my stories have shown you that if I can rise above racism, bullying, naysayers, and plenty of embarrassment to become a professional presenter, storyteller, and video expert, then you can become confident on camera and make videos that get many views too!

Don't walk – RUN towards your goals! You are worthy of all your wildest hopes and dreams and you have the power to make them happen. Focus on the amazing things that are ahead and shake off the distractions that try to pull you off course.

You and your story are worth sharing with the world. You can make a difference. Video is an important part of the puzzle that'll help get you and your story in front of the people who need it most.

Your time is now. Don't stay a secret.

With love and gratitude,

Felicia Yap

Felicia Yap

ACKNOWLEDGMENTS

Looking back at the whole experience of writing this book, one thing is clear: it was only made possible because of all the incredible people I have in my corner.

Lyndsie Barrie, I will never forget the time you told me that I should write a book. I didn't think I had what it takes to write a book until you planted that seed. Your amazing encouragement, advice and coaching have made all the difference in my book-writing journey.

Shane Fielder, from the moment I met you, you've wowed me with your world-class wisdom, expertise and brilliance. This book wouldn't be at the level that it is without your exceptional guidance.

My book cover designer, Cheryl Fielder, your stellar creative talent brought the vision of my book cover to life. It's everything I imagined and more.

Stephen Dutcher, I'm so grateful that you took on this project and shaped it with your standard of excellence and experience in editing. Both you and the quality of your work are impressive. I'm honoured that you've left your mark on this book.

Ryan Sang, you blew me away with your editorial feedback of this book. I knew when I asked you for help with the book that you would deliver, and you did not disappoint. Thank you for always being there for me. We may not be related by blood, but you are family.

Julia Wong, you are a word wizard. Thank you for sharing your superb gift of storytelling to help make this book what it is today. More importantly, thank you for your friendship. I can't wait for our next hangout.

My writing partner, Noreen Music, I could not think of a better person to have gone on this book journey with. You are a blessing in my life. I'm so proud of us for writing our first books together.

My cousin, Stephanie Lim, thanks for your endless encouragement, and for providing thorough feedback on every chapter of this book. You're an incredible human being who does so much good for so many people, including me and my family.

To my other cousin Yvonne Chapman, your courage to chase your dreams is inspiring. Thanks for generously sharing your insight and time in developing this book. I'm so proud of everything you've done and will do. Even though life has taken us on different paths and to different places, I always feel at home when we're together.

Having a true friend who believes in you and will help you review all the chapters in your book without a second thought is a gem. Mary Truong is that kind of friend to me. Mary, thank you for being someone I can count on and trust.

Jennifer Vuong, thanks for cheering me on during the creation of this book, and beyond. You've always been there for me with a hug and a heart-to-heart chat when I needed it.

Shane McQueen, I knew I asked the right person to help me with the audio section of this book. Your feedback and advice on the subject matter immediately put me at ease. Thank you for your eagerness and willingness to help. You are a class act.

One of my first bosses in broadcasting, Carl Worth, thank you for believing in me and giving me a shot. Your support during my formative years in the news industry means more to me than you'll ever know. You are a master of your craft, and I'm so glad I was able to learn from you when I did.

Cynthia Hamilton Urquhart, you helped me to grow as a writer by reminding me to "show, don't tell." Thank you for teaching me how to write with impact.

To my family who have watched me take every single step to create this book, you are the true MVPs. My younger brother, Shawn Yap, thanks for always being one of my greatest supporters. My older brother, Chris Yap, my mom and my dad, thank you all so much for taking care the girls without hesitation so I could work on the book. You give me the kind of support most moms would dream of, and I don't take that for granted.

Aurora and Gwyneth, I carry both of you in my heart everywhere I go. I hurt thinking about all the time I've spent away from you working on this book. I hope one day you'll see that Mama did all that work to create something important to help people, and that you'll be proud of me. I'm so proud of who you are and I'm excited to see who you will become. I love you both so much.

My rock and life partner, Andrew, you are my unicorn. I have to pinch myself when I think of all the amazing things you're doing and how much you love our family. Thank you for stepping up while I had to step aside to make this book happen. Thank you for pushing me to the finish line, even when I sometimes wanted to pull the plug. You make me a better person.

My clients and students, thank you for trusting me to tell your story, to help magnify your message, and to help you shine on camera. I'm honoured to be a part of your journey.

And lastly, Philippians 4:13.

NOTES

INTRODUCTION: A DENIAL DOES NOT MEAN DEFEAT

1. Steve Maraboli, "Unapologetically You: Reflections on Life and the Human Experience," 2013, www.goodreads.com/quotes/593861-life-is-too-short-to-waste-time-waiting-for-other.
2. Les Brown, *Quotefancy*, quotefancy.com/quote/853068/Les-Brown-You-cannot-be-wimpy-out-there-on-the-dream-seeking-trail-Dare-to-break-through.
3. Bryant McGill, *Quotefancy*, quotefancy.com/quote/779755/Bryant-McGill-Rejection-is-merely-a-redirection-a-course-correction-to-your-destiny.

CHAPTER 1: P.R.E.P. FOR SUCCESS

1. Michael Jordan, *Quotefancy*, quotefancy.com/quote/759012/Michael-Jordan-Get-the-fundamentals-down-and-the-level-of-everything-you-do-will.
2. NUTV, nutv.ca/about/.
3. Kim Gardner, "Quality is in the Eye of the Beholder: New Research on What Viewers Love," *Think with Google,* April 2019, www.thinkwithgoogle.com/marketing-strategies/video/video-production-quality/.
4. Shane McQueen, email to author, 14 January 2022.
5. Fred Shook, *Television Field Production and Reporting*, 4th ed. Allyn and Bacon, 2005.
6. "Different Types of Video Editing," *Mediacollege.com*, www.mediacollege.com/video/editing/tutorial/methods.html.

CHAPTER 2: BRING OUT THE BEST YOU

1. Oscar Wilde, *Goodreads*, www.goodreads.com/quotes/19884-be-yourself-everyone-else-is-already-taken.
2. "How to Overcome Perfectionism." *Anxiety* [WHY IS THERE A GAP HERE?]

Canada, www.anxietycanada.com/sites/default/files/Perfectionism.pdf.

3. Oscar Morley, *Quotetab*, www.quotetab.com/quote/by-robert-morley/to-fall-in-love-with-yourself-is-the-first-secret-to-happiness.
4. Jen Mueller, "5 Quotes to Inspire You to Find Your Voice," *Talk Sporty To Me*, 21 October 2020, www.talksportytome.com/blog/5-quotes-to-inspire-you-to-find-your-voice.
5. Lesley Childs, "Voice Care: Sorting Fact from Fiction," *UT Southwestern Medical Centre*, 14 April 2016, utswmed.org/medblog/vocal-cords-care-qa/.
6. P. Arias, P. Belin, and J.J. Aucouturier, "Auditory Smiles Trigger Unconscious Facial Imitation," *Current Biology*, 23 Jul 2018, 28(14):R782-R783. doi: 10.1016/j.cub.2018.05.084. Erratum in *Current Biology*, 20 Aug 2018, 28(16):2681-2683. PMID: 30040936.
7. "Why Do I Think Better after I Exercise?" *Scientific American*, 1 July 2013, www.scientificamerican.com/article/why-do-you-think-better-after-walk-exercise/.
8. "Why Do I Think Better after I Exercise?" *Scientific American.*, 1 July 2013, Karen Li, Instagram comment, *Instagram*, 25 August 2021, www.instagram.com/tv/CTA0Xaahh0a/?utm_medium=copy_link.
9. Jamie Kern Lima, *Believe It.* Gallery Books, 2021, p. 10.
10. Susan Sarandon, *BrainyQuote*, www.brainyquote.com/quotes/susan_sarandon_126075.

CHAPTER 3: HOW TO SET YOURSELF APART FROM EVERYONE ELSE

1. Steve Jobs, *Goodreads*, www.goodreads.com/quotes/772887-the-only-way-to-do-great-work-is-to-love.
2. Khalil Gibran, *BrainyQuote*, www.brainyquote.com/quotes/khalil_gibran_386848.

3. Kristin Hannah, *Goodreads*, www.goodreads.com/quotes/418544-finding-your-passion-isn-t-just-about-careers-and-money-it-s.
4. Ira Glass, *Goodreads*, www.goodreads.com/quotes/1317166-great-stories-happen-to-those-who-can-tell-them.
5. Loren Eiseley, "The Star Thrower," *Wikipedia*, en.wikipedia.org/wiki/The_Star_Thrower.
6. Marie Forleo, "THIS Made Me… x 1,000," email to author, 8 July 2021.
7. Eric J. Olson, "How Many Hours of Sleep are Enough for Good Health?" 15 May 2021, *Mayo Clinic*, www.mayoclinic.org/healthy-lifestyle/adult-health/expert-answers/how-many-hours-of-sleep-are-enough/faq-20057898.
8. Seth J. Gillihan, "The Healing Power of Telling Your Trauma Story: Six Ways Revisiting Painful Memories Can Loosen Their Grip," *Psychology Today*, 6 March 2019, www.psychologytoday.com/ca/blog/think-act-be/201903/the-healing-power-telling-your-trauma-story.

CHAPTER 4: YOUR STORIES IN YOUR STYLE

1. Margaret Atwood, "Inspiring Quotes on Storytelling," *Toastmasters International*, December 2019, www.toastmasters.org/magazine/magazine-issues/2019/dec/inspiring-quotes-on-storytelling.
2. Afton Brazzoni, interview by author, Zoom, 29 July 2021.

CHAPTER 5: HOW TO LIGHT UP A ROOM

1. John Ford, *Allauthor*, allauthor.com/quotes/126486/.
2. Lyndsie Barrie, interview by author, *Instagram*, 1 September 2021, www.instagram.com/tv/CTSzR45ClmP/?utm_source=ig_web_copy_link.
3. Noreen Music, interview by author, *Instagram*, 22 September 2021, www.instagram.com/tv/CUI57AXJggv/?utm_source=ig_web_copy_link.

CHAPTER 6: CAMERA-READY SECRETS

1. Will Rogers, *Goodreads*, www.goodreads.com/quotes/7515235-you-never-get-a-second-chance-to-make-a-first.
2. Laurie Brown, online correspondence with author, *Google Doc*, 20 November 2021.
3. Adrienne Furrie, interview by author, *Instagram*, 4 November 2021, www.instagram.com/tv/CV3cSPIJqBU/?utm_medium=copy_link.

CHAPTER 7: OVERCOMING CRITICISM AND CRICKETS

1. Bo Bennett, *CoolNSmart.com*, https://www.coolnsmart.com/quote-a-rejection-is-nothing-more-2-102333/.
2. Trevor Haynes, "Dopamine, Smartphones & You: A Battle for Your Time," Graduate School of Arts and Sciences, Harvard University, 1 May 2018, sitn.hms.harvard.edu/flash/2018/dopamine-smartphones-battle-time/.
3. *The Social Dilemma*, directed by Jeff Orlowski, Exposure Labs, Argent Pictures, The Space Program, 2020.
4. *Cognitive Behavioral Therapy Los Angeles*. "Common Cognitive Distortions: Negative Filtering, 5 June 2015, cogbtherapy.com/cbt-blog/common-cognitive-distortions-negative-filtering.
5. "Mean Tweets Live," YouTube, uploaded by *Jimmy Kimmel Live*, 24 September 2015, www.youtube.com/watch?v=LsKFsF2zpFM.
6. "Celebrities Read Mean Tweets #12," YouTube, uploaded by *Jimmy Kimmel Live*, 25 September 2019, www.youtube.com/watch?v=FLTOiQ8gXp4.
7. George Shaw, *BrainyQuote*, www.brainyquote.com/quotes/george_bernard_shaw_137450.
8. Center for Countering Digital Hate, *Don't Feed the Trolls: How to Deal with Hate on Social Media*,

2019, docs.wixstatic.com/ugd/f4d9b9_ce178075e9654b719ec2b4815290f00f.pdf.

9. Simone Elkeles, *Goodreads*, www.goodreads.com/quotes/590355-opinions-are-like-assholes-everybody-s-got-one-and-everyone-thinks.
10. Hillary Clinton, *Goodreads*, www.goodreads.com/quotes/102494-take-criticism-seriously-but-not-personally-if-there-is-truth.
11. Yvonne Chapman, interview by author, Zoom, 17 June 2021.

CHAPTER 8: YOU ARE THE REAL DEAL

1. Stan Smith, *Goodreads*, www.goodreads.com/quotes/243387-experience-tells-you-what-to-do-confidence-allows-you-to.
2. "Panic Disorder: When Fear Overwhelms," *National Institute of Mental Health*, 2016, www.nimh.nih.gov/health/publications/panic-disorder-when-fear-overwhelms/.
3. Pauline R. Clance, "Impostor Phenomenon," paulineroseclance.com/impostor_phenomenon.html.
4. J. Sakulku, "The Imposter Phenomenon," *Journal of Behavioral Science*, vol. 6, no. 1, 1, pp. 75-97, doi:10.14456/jibs.2011.6. so06.tci-thaijo.org/index.php/IJBS/article/view/521/pdf.
5. Valerie Young, "10 Steps You Can Use to Overcome Imposter Syndrome," https://impostorsyndrome.com/10-steps-overcome-impostor/.
6. Dale Carnegie, *Goodreads*, www.goodreads.com/quotes/1140103-inaction-breeds-doubt-and-fear-action-breeds-confidence-and-courage.
7. Glenn Halbrooks, "Get Higher Ratings With These TV Sweeps Tips," *The Balance Careers*, 2 June 2019, www.thebalancecareers.com/get-higher-ratings-with-these-tv-sweeps-tips-2315428.
8. Emily Chase, interview by author, *Instagram*, 4 June 2021.

CLOSING: PUTTING THE PIECES TOGETHER

1. Colin Powell, *BrainyQuote*, www.brainyquote.com/quotes/colin_powell_121363.

ABOUT THE AUTHOR

Felicia H. Yap is a professional videographer, speaker, content creator, and video confidence coach who began with nothing more than her dad's camcorder and a deep love for telling stories.

For the past 20 years, Felicia has worked on screen and behind the camera to help a whole gamut of story-makers share their unique message with the world. The former TV journalist has done it all as a news anchor, morning show co-host, reporter, videographer, producer, and weather specialist for CTV – one of Canada's largest news networks.

She stepped away from a successful career to pave her own path when she became a mom, launching her DIY YouTube channel, *Most Delightful Way* in 2015 and then founding Reel Awesome Productions in 2020 to help big-hearted business owners and professionals look and feel confident on camera. Whether you need video production services, interview preparation or video confidence coaching, Felicia can help you connect with your audience.

Felicia lives in Calgary, Alberta, Canada with her husband and their children.

Hire Felicia as a Speaker

Engaging. Entertaining. Professional. Inspirational.

With roughly 30 years of public speaking experience, Felicia has delivered speeches and emceed fundraisers in front of thousands of people.

Two of Felicia's signature talks include:

- Five ways to jumpstart your video confidence
- How to share your message with maximum impact

EMAIL FELICIA

HELLO@REELAWESOME.COM

Manufactured by Amazon.ca
Bolton, ON

24248027R00157